A BOY'S WAR

ALSO BY PAXTON DAVIS

Two Soldiers
The Battle of New Market
One of the Dark Places
The Seasons of Heroes
A Flag at the Pole
Ned
Three Days
Being a Boy

A BOY'S WAR

by Paxton Davis

JOHN F. BLAIR, PUBLISHER
WINSTON-SALEM, NORTH CAROLINA

This book is printed on acid-free paper.

Library of Congress Cataloging-in-Publication Data
Davis, Paxton, 1925–
A boy's war / by Paxton Davis.
p. cm.
ISBN 0–89587–079–7 (acid-free) :
1. Davis, Paxton, 1925– —Biography—Youth.
2. Journalists—United States—Biography.
3. World War, 1939–1945—Personal narrative, American. I. Title.
PN4874.D374A3 1990
070'.92—dc20
[B]
90–970

For

Ira Singer, Bob Austrian,
Frogg Kailey and Caroline Clegg

and
in loving memory for

Gene Hughes

I am deeply grateful to The MacDowell Colony
for a term of residence in which to complete this book;
and to the late Robert Penn Warren,
who first called my attention to the
Melville poem from which its title is drawn.

A BOY'S WAR

Did all the lets and bars appear
To every just or larger end,
Whence should come the trust and cheer?
Youth must its ignorant impulse lend—
Age finds place in the rear.
All wars are boyish, and are fought by boys,
The champions and enthusiasts of the state . . .

from Melville's
"March into Virginia"
Battle Pieces

i

Pubescent boys can hardly be said to think at all, let alone to hold anything so intangible as an idea; and when the United States finally entered World War II in December 1941 I was as surprised as everyone else. By then the portents of war had been powerful for most of my boyhood, especially since Hitler's annexation of Austria in 1937. I could vividly remember the actual outbreak of general European war in September 1939, when, returning at fourteen from my first trip to New York, I found myself across the street from the White House as my bus stopped for newspaper extras screaming the German invasion of Poland. But like most Americans, and like boys of any country, I had registered the brilliant images of great events without allowing myself to understand their significance. I was as fascinated by violence as anyone, but the violence I knew was the fantasy violence of movies and books; the daily life I actually knew was calm, orderly and peaceful, as island America with its two sea walls was, and behind those formidable protections against the true violence of the world I lived in a daydream. It was inconceivable to me that I might have to surrender the sweetness, safety and innocence of my boyhood to a war in distant Europe and Asia.

Yet the war came anyway. I was fifteen the following spring when the Nazi panzers overran Denmark, Norway and the Low Countries, then plunged into France and forced its surrender in the same railway car in which Germany had surrendered in 1918. The next summer, when I was sixteen, Hitler turned on Russia, and before winter had begun the Japanese attack on Pearl Harbor, regarded by most Americans as their unassailable fortress guarding the Pacific, brought the United States into the war, the event we'd all convinced ourselves would never occur.

By then I was a senior at R. J. Reynolds High School in Winston-Salem, North Carolina, and even then, with real war an actuality, with American soldiers and sailors already losing their lives and with many older friends, acquaintances and relatives already in uniform, I was confident, as all my close friends were, that it would never reach me. My adored Uncle Stuart McDowell, the second of my mother's three younger brothers, was a 1925 graduate of the Virginia Military Institute and an officer in the Army Reserve—he'd been summoned to active duty a year before and as a field artillery captain was training mountain troops in Colorado. Nick Dimling, who lived next door and was ten years older than I, had been one of the first to be called in the draft of 1940 and was finishing Officers Candidate School at Fort Benning; he seemed to me almost mythically heroic with his shoulders gleaming beneath the gold bars of a second lieutenant of infantry. Charles Speas, six years older than I, had been commissioned by way of the Reserve Officers Training Corps upon his graduation from M.I.T. and had long since gone on active duty as an ordnance officer. Down the block Frank Clingman, a strapping recent journalism graduate of the University of North Carolina, was serving as an officer in the Coast Guard. Even my father, in his midfifties and a weathered veteran of World War I, was flirting with another stint of active service. Because of his expertise as head of trucking for the Reynolds Tobacco Company the War Department had offered him a commission as lieutenant colonel in the Transportation Corps with the assignment of developing and commanding a new truck regiment. Only my mother's objections and the company's unwillingness to let him go finally dissuaded him from accepting. He was a singularly handsome man who always dressed and bore himself beautifully, and I was crushed that I would not get to see him, dashing and glamorous, in olive blouse and pinks.

These romantic vaporings not only reveal my innocence but typify the way by which my generation of American boys kept knowledge of the true nature of war at as safe a distance as we could contrive. My father, like my friend Grady Southern's father, warned us that the war in France had been wholly unlike the movies we doted on, death bloodier and almost never wrapped in the noble sentiments displayed, say, by Jimmy Cagney in *The Fighting 69th*; but we clung to the heroics on-screen. They made war both valiant, which it rarely is, and beautiful, which as Robert E. Lee observed is one of its most dangerous seductions; for we wanted at all costs to preserve the warm security in which we had passed the enchanted time of boyhood. I had lived since birth in Winston-Salem, a small, prosperous and attractive Southern city whose working life revolved around the manufacture of cigarettes, underwear and ladies' hose, on a serene street of shade trees, deep lawns and big, comfortable houses at the heart of a suburb that was a citadel of upper-middle-class privilege and affluence. It was a neighborhood of doctors and lawyers and company executives, like my father and Grady's, and it was thronged with boys my own age or thereabouts. Everyone knew everyone else, and parents praised or admonished each other's children without fear of repercussion, safe in the knowledge that all of them shared the same essential notions of what was right and wrong, what the good life should be and what should be done to hold their children to the standard necessary to its achievement. My closest friends were Grady, who lived down the block, and Tommy and Freddy Speas, the latter three years older than we, who were the younger of the five brilliant sons of the city's leading ophthalmologist. Dozens of other boys lived within a stone's throw and all of us were the sort of friends only boys can be who have done everything together—from battling in the dust to playing football and baseball until dark year after year to going to the movies, school and summer camp—almost since leaving the cradle. Our parents had maids and cooks, served us good food of which there was always enough for another chair at the table and saw to it that we dressed well, were seen by the doctor when hurt or feverish, went to church Sundays, camp summers, school daily and did our homework before going to bed. Crime was unknown and cars few, and because they were our lives were snug in a freedom from danger hardly imaginable today. We did not want, I think, to grow up.

Life proceeded, that spring of 1942, along parallel tracks that proved in retrospect to have been running in opposite directions. In the more familiar one I was a sixteen-year-old boy doing all the things adolescents of that simple time did as they neared the end of high school. I was admitted to college for the fall. I made the varsity tennis team at last and, after a season of eleven wins and nine losses, won my large black-and-gold "WS" monogram, in which I took inordinate pride. In "Miss Mary" Wiley's homeroom English class I outraged her by reading Sinclair Lewis, whom she sternly detested, and writing my papers and test in a tiny, cramped hand, which she sternly disliked. I performed meaningless experiments in my basement chemistry laboratory and dreamed of winning an early

Nobel Prize. Finding my clothes too short and too tight, I discovered to my astonishment and delight that I'd grown two inches in a year and now stood a towering five-foot-eight—scarcely making me tall in the way Grady was, or many others, but liberating me from runthood. With that step into the real world I took another, finding that I had simultaneously lost my shyness with girls and fallen in love. Her name was Nancy Smitherman, she was a classmate in Miss Mary's, she lived in Ardmore and she had everything I could dream of: beauty, brains, startling blue eyes, lustrous long brown hair and a limitless reservoir of good-humored patience for my apparently incurable awkwardness whenever I was around her. I tripped over furniture, tumbled off her front-porch steps, repeatedly stalled my father's '36 Oldsmobile coupe on the rare occasions I was allowed to use it and never remembered to wear a raincoat even in the heaviest showers; but she simply smiled, those blue eyes twinkling, and set me back on whatever path I'd lost. No one had much money and gas was already being rationed, so most of our dates consisted of walking, on warm spring evenings, to Bobbitt's Pharmacy at "the Foot" of Ardmore Hill, where I regularly followed the purchase of two Cokes by spilling my change all over the floor. Sunday nights, once it was clear we were going steady, we met after our separate churches' "young people's" meetings and walked to Betsy Long's weekly open house in West End; she was a sensational belle our own age whose parents generously threw open their big Victorian house to dozens of boys and girls who passed their inspection. There we drank soft drinks obligingly supplied by Betsy's father, who owned the Big Boy Cola plant, and listened to Tommy Dorsey on the record player, mooning with moist eyes over "I'll Never Smile Again," "Swanee River" and that season's sentimental wartime hit, "Last Call for Love." Afterward we walked a couple of miles to her house, daringly holding hands down the dark streets, and then I had to walk a couple of miles farther to get home. It was as innocent as Eden before the Fall, and just as sweet. She wore my Hi-Y pin, and once she let me kiss her goodnight; I saved the handkerchief bearing her lipstick for years.

The parallel track moved toward a harsher future. Even as the last months of high school unfolded Japan's conquest of the Pacific approached its culmination. In the central Pacific chain after chain of hitherto exotic islands were overrun and occupied. Manila fell; Bataan fell, then Corregidor, and the collapse of the Philippines was complete. Invasion of Australia appeared imminent. Meanwhile Hong Kong surrendered, and then Singapore, its guns turned immovably seaward as the Japanese poured down the Malay Peninsula, costing the loss of thousands of British soldiers and sailors doomed to brutal imprisonment, torture and sometimes execution by their unforgiving captors. Still farther west, threatening India and raising the ominous prospect of an Axis-Mideast conjunction, the Japanese conquered Rangoon and Burma filled up with Japanese invaders south to north, the only redeeming feature of its defeat a heroic exodus of British, Indian and American troops who walked out to India across hideous jungle and mountains under the peppery leadership of an American general named Joseph W. Stilwell. In Assam he told the press, unlike the boastful MacArthur, "We got a hell of a licking . . . " I'd never heard of him and had to go to an atlas to find Burma.

Those events were to play a crucial role in my future, but I sensed no hint of it. I loved tennis, spring, Nancy, the good life of my family, neighborhood and hometown; and on the June night of my graduation from Reynolds High School I was euphoric with the thought of them all and the prospect of entering college in September. After the graduation dance ended in the small morning hours I took Nancy home and delivered newspapers on Buena Vista Road and Oaklawn Avenue before going to bed, irreparably blackening my white jacket with newsprint as I went. The stars were still bright and a heavy dew glistened against the trees and shrubs of my route; it was inconceivable that so serene a peace could ever end. I was seventeen; a few months earlier America had lowered its draft age to eighteen.

ii

I was in the army for three years during World War II, in uniform four. The difference was the year I spent at V.M.I., which in most respects proved more hazardous and in all respects more difficult.

When I entered it in September 1942 the Virginia Military Institute was only three years more than a century old. It was, as it remains today, an academic institution unusually combining what usually seem disparate—perhaps even contradictory—features: on one side an undergraduate college offering bachelor's degrees in a conventional range of scholarly and professional disciplines, on the other a military post under whose tutelage every undergraduate was trained to the most demanding standards of professional martial accomplishment. The goal of the school was, from its inception, the creation of "citizen soldiers" who are prepared at any moment, like Cincinnatus, to drop the plow to take up the sword. Operated by the Commonwealth of Virginia, which founded it in 1839 to replace a state militia arsenal at the same site, it bestrides a rocky crag overlooking the Maury River along the northern border of Lexington, also the home of Washington & Lee University, whose campus it abuts. Its stark physical eminence provoked at least one critic to observe that it was "built on a bluff and run on the same principle."

Thanks to its provenance, Virginia's enduring love of uniforms and military glory and its romantic part in the Civil War—Stonewall Jackson taught physics and tactics until 1861, numerous graduates had won high rank and reputation as Confederate officers by Appomattox and the Corps of Cadets had the distinction of being the only student body in history to face combat as a unit—V.M.I. was an institution most Southerners regarded as invincibly elite. Members of my family had attended it from the first: a great-great-grandfather, numerous cousins, most visibly all three of my mother's brothers, parts of whose old uniforms, particularly Stuart's shako, could still be discovered in the trunk room of my grandparents' big house in Fincastle, Virginia, where my sister and I spent the summers of our early childhood. I could not imagine going anywhere else to college, a sentiment Stuart and his older brother James McDowell, V.M.I. '17, took pains to encourage, driving me often to Lexington to watch Final Parade or one of the mounted reviews, displaying cavalry and field artillery units as well as the usual infantry formation, which were a glamorous, if in truth by then anachronistic, aspect of life on "the Post" during the 1930s.

Going to V.M.I. was thus a family ritual and seemed as inevitable to me as it did to my uncles and father, who as a boy had dreamed in vain of being a cadet himself—but not to Mother. Superbly educated in her own right, as well as wise about my nature and needs, she'd learned from watching her brothers to suspect deeply V.M.I.'s brutal creed of muscular masculinity, and she urged me to aim higher, or what was higher to her: Davidson, which she loved, or Hampden-Sydney, to which she pointedly reminded me her youngest brother, Turner, had happily transferred after two years at V.M.I., or even Princeton, to which she ascribed the highest attainments of American education. All of these, she maintained, boasted far more searching academic programs than V.M.I., not to mention far more distinguished alumni, and the opportunities they offered for the kind of intellectual development of which she believed me capable were far greater. That all were strongly Presbyterian, either historically or traditionally, she dismissed as coincidence—though I was not fooled and accused her, with some heat, of trying secretly to turn me into a Presbyterian minister. She knew me better than I knew myself, I realized afterward, but that spring she was simply no match for son, husband and brothers. Turner, who'd left V.M.I. for Hampden-Sydney, was regarded as the family apostate and remained silent.

Having a good high-school record and voluminous family ties guaranteed me early acceptance, and the fact that my father could afford the steep tab assessed out-of-state cadets did not hurt. I got my letter of appointment by return mail, whereupon James, then living briefly in Winston-Salem on leave from his job in Greece, remarked drily, "I hope you're ready for the Rat line." Till then, I suddenly realized, I had regarded that notorious custom as a trifle.

It was no trifle. The wonderful summer—work as a laboratory assistant at the Bowman Gray School of Medicine, daily tennis with Grady, evenings of movies and walks with Nancy—passed in the sort of golden daze all adolescents know; and suddenly September saw me lugging a decrepit old suitcase stuffed with the requisite white shirts, T-shirts, boxer shorts and black socks, as well as a pair of garters I had no idea how to use, up the hill from the Lexington Greyhound bus stop to face at last the gray, forbidding fortress of V.M.I.—not the Camelot of my romantic daydreams but the V.M.I. of reality—and it was terrifying.

V.M.I. discipline, of which it boasted constantly, was and is founded on terror, which began the moment a new cadet, or "Rat," entered barracks immediately after signing in just outside. Barracks, the center of cadet life, was an immense gray quadrangle, appropriately crenellated and entered through two towered arches, whose four stories, or "stoops," held all cadet rooms, one stoop to a class, with Rats at the top, seniors, or "first classmen," on the ground. A cadet sentry stood guard beside a sentry box in the courtyard, and steel staircases led upward at each of its four interior corners. A Rat was required to enter by a straight line and to follow it thereafter, rounding all corners by the longest possible outside route, running up all stairs and bracing, shoulders back, chin and gut in, as rigidly as he could be made to, so that a Rat's first experience of V.M.I. was to walk the immemorial "Rat line" to the loud, ceaseless braying of senior cadets lining the stoops. To them he was "Mister," sometimes "Misto," and though they were forbidden to strike or even touch him he was expected to obey their most whimsical or most brutal commands instantly and unquestioningly—everything from shining his shoes or going for cigarettes at the Post Exchange to reciting parts of the Rat catechism ("Who won the Civil War, Mister?" "V.M.I. with the aid of the South, sir") and bracing in place, or "finning out," behind the door. All of this was ritual, a conception of education based on harassment and fear, and it continued without pause throughout most of a cadet's first year.

Within minutes of reaching his assigned room and dropping his bags a Rat was set in motion: issued a V.M.I. cap, pale blue denim fatigue trousers, a gray flannel shirt, web belt and high-topped black shoes; measured by tailors for permanent uniform, in those days made on the post; given a closer haircut than he had dreamed possible; issued a .30-calibre Springfield rifle and bayonet, model 1903; and marched in a six-man squad onto the huge grassy parade ground, the "Hill," to learn the rudiments of close-order drill as well as such fundamental military practices as saluting and standing at attention, which for a wiggly seventeen-year-old boy like me was not as easy as it looked. After a day or two I could not help noticing that some of my new classmates, my "Brother Rats," caught on at once while others, including me, shed their awkwardness only with difficulty. The difference was that more than a few, especially the "army brats," had attended military prep school, A.M.A., Staunton, Greenbriar, Fishburne, Culver, before entering V.M.I. In martial smartness, in fact, they kept ahead of the rest of us for most of our time as Rats—a tiny advantage, but a crucial one, that I was able to exploit in turn a year later as a soldier.

That advantage did not extend to the classroom. The Rat academic curriculum was virtually uniform—English composition, European history, college algebra, a modern language, a science—and under such egalitarian circumstances it quickly became clear that some new cadets were far better prepared, perhaps more generously endowed by nature, than others. Virtually all V.M.I. classes, chemistry lectures apart, were small, usually limited to sections of ten or twelve; and in them, as had been the custom at West Point, Annapolis and V.M.I. from their earliest days, every member was expected to recite or write at every meeting. In most courses this meant literally going to the blackboard to solve equations, parse irregular verbs, diagram complex sentences or demonstrate difficult chemical reactions, all under the critical eye of an instructor who, to make matters worse, taught in officer's uniform. This daily drill, though elementary, soon separated the quick from the dull, for it left the poorly prepared little time to ponder and no time to seek a classmate's help. Some of my most eager parade-ground Brother Rats promptly showed that they would never be more than mediocre in the classroom, while I and a few others discovered to our surprise and relief that, at least academically, we were likely to shine. This rapid winnowing was further accelerated by V.M.I.'s policy of posting all grades in all courses for all classes in barracks every other week, and of calculating from them every cadet's class standing in precise numerical order. As a result, everyone knew where he stood at all times—and so did everyone else. It was to V.M.I.'s everlasting credit, in fact, that, as conspicuously as it rewarded military and athletic excellence, it also made certain, by means of awards and announcements and bright gold stars on blouse and dress coatee, that intellectual attainment got the recognition it deserved.

Competent instruction could be found at V.M.I., and occasionally the level of pedagogy rose higher. History was inexcusably dull in the classrooms of Colonels Fuller and Townes, who was known as "Nero" and had a lisp widely imitated in barracks, but my English classes with Major Carrington Tutwiler, who was Ellen

Glasgow's nephew and a recent Ph.D. from Princeton, were remarkable. He was a superb grammarian who used drill in composition as a vehicle not only to drum clarity and order into stubborn Rat minds but also to enlarge their familiarity with English and American literature, a lot of which was assigned us well before it officially entered the curriculum. As a boy in grammar and high schools, constantly spurred by my mother's conviction that writing was my special gift, I had always written easily and abundantly; but at V.M.I. Tutwiler's sometimes lordly tutelage revealed for me not only the utility of prose but its power and majesty, and I did so well at English, ending the year with a standing of second among more than two hundred, that I began to feel a strong, perhaps even professional, pull in that direction. Among others whose teaching seemed to me superior that year were Major Riley Horne, who did as much as human nature could to make my math proficient, and a young civilian instructor named Norman Binger, who briefly aroused my interest in introductory German.

Yet they and other instructors of more than routine skill paled, in V.M.I.'s general atmosphere, alongside the overwhelming look and sound and spirit of what is nowadays called *machismo*. In the end, both physically and emotionally, V.M.I. worshipped male prowess. Athletics bore an astonishing importance, and on the individual and intramural as well as intercollegiate levels. Rat physical education was daily and demanding, derived from the training given navy aviators at flight schools, besides which Rats were required not only to attend all home intercollegiate contests in all sports but to participate actively in the intramural matches, organized by cadet companies, in touch football, basketball, wrestling and softball. Small and slender, I took modest gratification in discovering that in wrestling, where one competed by weight, I could at least hold my own. As overheated as V.M.I.'s obsession with sports was, however, it seemed almost cool when compared to the military spirit permeating every aspect of life on the post. Every cadet was in one or another of the numerous combinations of uniform at all times, and for much of the time he was performing a military task. But so were virtually all of the administration, faculty and staff. Major General Charles E. Kilbourne, superintendent (i.e., president), had won the Medal of Honor and the Distinguished Service Cross before 1900 as well as supervised the construction of American defenses on Corregidor, and, with his white hair, frosted eyeglass, cane and slim, erect bearing, he was a striking and formidable figure as he crossed the parade ground between his quarters and office. Colonel John Fray, commandant and thus senior active army officer, was an old cavalryman who wore riding breeches and spurred boots most of the time and rode daily; he kept his hair cropped to an inch and gave his orders in a gruff voice most cadets tried to avoid. Another grizzled cavalryman was Colonel John Caperton, who taught me to ride (no simple task), and a recent V.M.I. graduate, Lieutenant Flournoy

Barksdale, universally known as "Pinky" because of his florid coloring, supervised much Rat instruction in military matters. But even the academic faculty, few of whom had a military background and none of whom was on active duty, were in uniform too, as officers of the Virginia Militia (Unorganized), and wore appropriate badges of rank: full professors were colonels, associate professors lieutenant colonels, assistant professors majors, and so on. No distinction was drawn between their status and the status of the army officers actually stationed at V.M.I. as part of their duty, and cadets were required to treat them with the same military punctilio, saluting them in passing and always addressing them by their ranks, though occasionally, noticing their inevitably casual indifference to the niceties of military dress, bearing and custom, we had to smile. Colonel W. M. Hunley, who was head of liberal arts and known as "College Bill," returned salutes by waving his cigar, and "Nero" Townes, though a decorated veteran of World War I, seemed something less than heroic when he took a section report with open fly or reproved a cadet for work he termed "grothly defithient."

Daily life was shaped by military procedure and marked by bugle and the regular beat of marching feet. Cadets awoke before dawn to the barracks bugler's "first call," then moved, minute by minute, to the increasing urgency of "reveille," "big toot" and "little toot" and thus, in a final rush, down the stoops and stairs to the first company formation of the day in front of the south and west sides of barracks. From there, preceded by roll calls of squads, platoons, companies and the two battalions that made up the regiment of the Corps of Cadets, they marched in perfect order down the hill to Crozet Hall for breakfast—a turbulent meal for Rats, who, usually still groggy, were expected not only to sit and eat at attention on the front inch of their chairs but to see to it that the glasses, coffee cups and plates of the upperclassmen around them were replenished on command. After tidying rooms they fell into new formations for class sections, always marching to every new class meeting; and that lasted, hour by hour, till noon, when the Corps formed again for lunch and a second march to the mess hall. The early afternoon went to labs, phys ed and military classes, to all of which cadets marched in sections; but at four the entire Corps marched onto the parade ground for an hour of close-order drill, followed at five by a change into full dress and an hour-long parade in which an elaborate ballet, probably little changed since Napoleon's day, culminated in the Corps' passing in review, company by company and platoon by platoon, before the critical eyes of the first captain and his staff to the wheezing oom-pah-pah of the post band, a makeshift assemblage of tailors and cooks known, in honor of the famous comic strip, as the "Toonerville Twelve." Dinner formation was next, the final roll call of the day; and the evening, reserved for study, ended with "tattoo" at ten-thirty and "taps" at eleven, whereupon barracks fell dark.

This relentless routine was rigid, rarely broken except on Wednesday, Saturday and Sunday afternoons, when cadets were allowed a few hours to go to a movie or have a soda at McCrum's drugstore or to ride the beautiful countryside on one of the more than two hundred cavalry and artillery mounts stabled on the post. No doubt to compensate for this show of permissiveness the powers decreed that a dress inspection must precede the Monday parade, a room and personal inspection Sunday morning before church. And it probably is unnecessary to add that church attendance was mandatory, though cadets were free to choose their denominations, or that they marched there in the usual formations through the streets of Lexington, giving their marching commands special emphasis as they passed the fraternity houses holding the sleeping students of neighboring Washington & Lee University. It remains to report that the largest section attended the fundamentalist Associate Reformed Presbyterian Church, not from any special piety for the faith of that sect, alas, but because its service was notoriously shorter than those of the mainstream Presbyterian, Episcopal, Baptist and Methodist churches. What Jewish cadets did in that overpoweringly Waspish environment, Corps and community alike, I never knew.

Underlying all this martial hustle, and inseparable from the V.M.I. ethos, was the Rat system. Its most visible feature was the Rat line, with its comic exaggeration of military posture and courtesy; what no one foreign to barracks saw was the grinding and ultimately demoralizing effect the hour-long, day-long, year-long bullying of Rats had on not only its victims but its perpetrators. Inspected by cadet corporals as they stood in ranks at all company formations, Rats delinquent in the smallest detail of correctness—shoes less than perfectly shined, brass less than perfectly polished, hair a milligram too long, the slightest stain from food or mud on cuff—inevitably resulted in a demerit or, worse, a command to report to "company room," a nightly ritual, following dinner, in which third classmen, or sophomores, spent most of an hour making Rats "fin out" in some corporal's room. To "fin out" required a rigid brace with knees bent, often with a corporal bellowing threats or blowing smoke in the culprit's face, and when it was over the exhausted Rat was likely to find the evening's study difficult. But any third classman, who was, after all, last year's Rat, could haze any Rat at any time, and many did, halting Rats as they passed on the stoop and ordering them, with rough authority, to do this or do that: close a window, buff a breastplate, shine a shoe, run an errand. Any upperclassman had the same unchecked power, for that matter, and though running the Rats was primarily a third-class prerogative, second- and first-class cadets often pitched in too. Every Rat "dyked" a first classman, helped tidy his room at reveille, helped him into his dress gear before parade, and the rationale was that such personal service gave the new cadet a protective "big brother" in the Corps, as it often did, though the older cadet and his roommates frequently behaved instead as if they were the powerful masters of a helpless serf. The Rat line could be dangerous and it was always frightening, for no Rat ever knew what capricious barbarity he might meet from one moment to the next; but no serious effort to moderate its abuses, let alone to replace it in favor of a program of indoctrination that encouraged self-discipline, ever went far. The Rat system "bred men," it was argued, "taught obedience," "instilled respect," "created class unity"; and administrators and faculty, many of them products of the same tradition, solemnly accepted such nonsense. The truth was that the Rat line was a form of authorized sadism in which one class imposed on its successors precisely the harshness and terror it had endured the year before; and all it taught was that might makes right, that brutality works. That reasoning, an insult to the developing mind and personality, implies that learning is built on fear, that the most important lesson in life is obedience to authority, however arbitrary; but its consequence, rarely admitted, is that both parties end by being debased. The common result is not a refinement but a coarsening of character. V.M.I. fostered and enshrined a perpetual male adolescence and its crudest values. The calendar stood steady at 1850.

But if V.M.I. was a muscum piece, a nineteenth-century artifact, beyond the historic Limits Gates through which one entered the post the world was on the march to rougher rhythms than the measured cadences of the Corps of Cadets. During my Rat year

American infantry and armor invaded French North Africa, were fighting and dying for the Kasserine Pass and moved toward the invasion of Sicily and then Italy, while across the world combined American forces began pushing westward through the central and south Pacific: the Solomon Islands, Tarawa, New Guinea, Bougainville, the Gilberts. At V.M.I. I learned to fire a Colt .45 automatic from the back of a galloping horse, the crucial lesson being that hitting the target was less important than missing the horse; it was a skill I would not be asked to display in the years that followed. Faces began to vanish from barracks: here and there deferments lapsed, and then, suddenly, a third of the Rat class, those already eighteen or more, were called to active duty from the Enlisted Reserve Corps. We younger ones waited, but only briefly. On May 7, 1943, I turned eighteen and registered for the draft at the Rockbridge County Courthouse in Lexington. The academic year, what would prove to be my only year at V.M.I., ended with the customary pomp and dash two weeks later.

I left profoundly and permanently ambivalent about the experience. Part of me took an almost platitudinous male pride in surviving V.M.I.'s ceaseless rigors without flinching, crying or quitting. Though no larval Patton, I had done well enough in ranks to get by and even, at the end, to win promotion to corporal in "C" Company—the lowest-ranking corporal of all, to be sure, but stripes were stripes. I was grateful for the excellent instruction I'd received in English and satisfied that the rest of my courses—except, ironically, for military science—had been adequate. But another part of me resented the pride and saw its shallowness; much of V.M.I. had proved, as Mother had foreseen, mean and petty as well as archaic and useless, and those had no part, to my mind, in genuine education. If my blood warmed to the bugles and drums, my mind despised them and the dark underside of human nature they symbolized.

I had little time to ponder such thoughts, however. Within a week of going home to Winston-Salem I was called to take my preliminary physical. A week after that I was classified 1-A.

iii

Physical standards for army induction in 1943 were nowhere near as high as the public was led to believe—I was to train and serve with men whose hernias, punctured eardrums, rotten teeth and missing eyes would have made them 4-F had they come from Hollywood—and such limitations often made army duty painful and difficult for the soldiers who bore them. My feelings on leaving V.M.I. were a tangle of contradictions, but for at least one result of my year there I was grateful: thanks to the incessant demands of phys ed, drill, parade, intramural sports and the Rat line I was in glowing condition, the best, I expect, of my life, for though small and thin I was wiry and tireless, with stamina and reserve V.M.I. had produced in me whether I liked it or not.

With steady tennis, biking, walking and swimming I was able to hold that edge as the hot summer passed. It passed slowly. Once I'd been marked 1-A I expected to be called at any moment; what I did not know, and what the country was not told, was that conscription was proceeding so effectively that the induction centers through which draftees entered the armed forces had become logjammed with recruits, to the point where local quotas had to be lowered until the glut had been absorbed into training camps. Voluntary enlistments had long since been halted in favor of the more predictable draft, but for several months in the spring and summer of 1943 the system provided more servicemen than the services could handle—a level of efficiency I was not to witness again.

I spent the early summer waiting for something to happen, working halfheartedly at my old laboratory job, playing tennis with men above draft age, dating Nancy, and was richly unhappy. My closest friends, being months older, were already in uniform: Tommy Speas was in an Army Signal Corps school at the University of Virginia, where I went to spend a weekend with him; Grady Southern was in an army camp somewhere down South training, because of his size and strength, to be an MP; Freddy Speas, three years older, had learned on his examination for the U.S. Naval Reserve that he had leukemia, but with the valor that never deserted him he determined to proceed with his medical career and, now somehow accepted by the navy, was busily pursuing his first-year studies at the

Bowman Gray School of Medicine in Winston-Salem, where we sometimes passed in the halls. But I was anxious and took it out on my parents and sister and Nancy, with all of whom I was cross. The truth was that I was not only miserable at the uncertainty but embarrassed to be, as I thought, the only male between twelve and sixty still wearing civvies.

The wait was briefer than it seemed. By the first of August I had received the president's greetings and within a few days was on a chartered Greyhound bus, with fifty or sixty other Winston-Salem men, bound for Camp Croft, an army base a few miles outside Spartanburg, South Carolina. Croft was a large camp serving a variety of purposes, but the only one concerning us was that of an induction center for most of the Carolinas. Induction was, like many army operations, a fixed and unvarying assembly-line procedure by which potential draftees selected by their local boards were sorted by doctors and interviewers into those who met conscription standards and those who did not. The former were sworn, offered GI insurance, given temporary papers, assigned a serial number they were urged to memorize at once and sent home, in the same bus that had brought them, for three weeks' final furlough to put their affairs in order. We were herded and handled like prisoners: set on the process immediately, confined to the induction area and moved mechanically from one step to the next. It all took less than twenty-four hours.

The first and most important step, overriding everything, was the physical examination, which was given to us and hundreds of others that day in a large open-frame building, as cavernous as a gymnasium and just as private. Along the wall beside the entrance hooks awaited our clothing, all of it, and as soon as we were undressed we lined up, stark-naked Southern males of startlingly diverse size, build, hue, musculature, posture and condition, at the first examination post, a row of small tables at which we gave brief medical histories. From there, one by one in what looked like an endless line, we moved from post to post: sticking out our tongues, baring our teeth, having light beams aimed at our eyegrounds, having our chests percussed and listened to and blood pressures taken, our groins examined by flashlight, our rear ends spread and studied, our calves and ankles and feet felt; we gave urine and blood. It was reassuring, I suppose, to learn that I displayed no abnormalities of eyes, ears, lungs or heart and that I was innocent of crabs, clap, pox, hemorrhoids, varicose veins and flat feet; but though accustomed to the nudity of locker rooms and V.M.I. showers I was unprepared for the raw spectacle of so many men undergoing so many simultaneous indignities in public view, so many invasions of their most intimate parts and functions. Until that moment my life had been privileged and protected; I did not like exposing myself to doctors I'd never met, to rednecks of whose existence I'd never dreamed; I wanted to hide behind a post, to run for cover. Instead I got my first army lesson: there were no posts, no cover—as everyone said repeatedly in those days, this was it.

But not quite. The final stop—by then we'd dressed again—was a row of cubicles for psychiatrists. I'd heard of Freud, most of it sex chat, but knew as little about psychiatry as I did about the dark side of the moon, and the man I drew, a dumpy, grumpy, rumpled captain in sweat-soaked suntans, looked as foreign to me as a Houyhnhnm. He asked with a leer if I liked girls, to which I gave an enthusiastic "Yes," then whether I got along with my parents, to which I gave an uncomprehending nod. At that he sprang. "Ever walk in your sleep?" "Sure," I said, "once or twice when I was little." He leaned across the table separating us. "You telling the truth?" "Yes, sir," I said, puzzled at his sudden interest. "Then you're rejected, son"—whereupon, marking my papers and handing them back, he looked up and said, "Next man. Move on."

Rejected? I couldn't believe it; I wouldn't; but the non-coms and officers collecting papers at the end of the line took one look and waved me past. *Rejected?* To the last man nearest the door, a staff sergeant who looked halfway human, I said, "I don't get it. How come?" He said, "Standard procedure. Guard duty. Afraid you'll wander off some night and get everybody in trouble." "But I was just a *kid*," I said, "It was years ago." He nodded. "Tell you what. Go back and get some affidavits from your doctor, maybe a teacher or preacher." He paused, eyed me curiously for the first time. "You don't mean you want to get *in* this fucking army? The rest of us want to get *out*." "I sure as hell don't want to stay home," I told him.

By the time I got there the next night I was in agony. My parents assured me we'd start collecting statements first thing in the morning; my father would exact a promise from the draft board to return me to Camp Croft on the next quota. But I was inconsolable. I was the only boy in the old neighborhood gang the army wouldn't have. I was the only living American who'd finish college on schedule. The rest of my life I'd be branded a slacker, a draft dodger. I was ruined—not because I'd walked in my sleep at the age of five, which till then I'd assumed everybody did, but because I hadn't had the gumption to lie about it. "It'll work out," Daddy said. "Never," I said. "They'll probably put a big red C on my chest. C for coward."

"Cowardice" is a questionable concept, difficult to define and impossible to apply, and whether I was or am guilty of it I still do not know. But in the climate of 1943 failure to serve in the armed forces inflicted a stigma, for a white male of my age, to be feared and loathed. Twenty years later many young Americans of privileged position and educational advantage showed no shame in using whatever loopholes existed in conscription law to avoid the hazards of Vietnam, while others, some for reasons of conscience, some because their deferments were denied or had lapsed, fled to Canada, leaving the war to be fought by the few who felt the call of traditional patriotism or the many, black, poor, devoid of privilege and education, who could not seek or win deferment. The youth of my generation enjoyed no such moral luxury: a few won the status of conscientious objector honorably and either went to prison or accepted non-combatant war work. A few others, noticeable then and unforgettable now, sought and got deferments to attend medical school, though their desire to be doctors was new. The overwhelming rest—enough, by war's end, to have put sixteen million men under arms—went into uniform and wore it proudly (though uttering a silent daily prayer that the war would soon end and get them out of it). No one wanted to be regarded as a shirker or "coward," even if uncertain, in those moments of private candor we all have, what "cowardice" really is.

My dread would have been felt by almost anyone finding himself in my plight, in other words; but it did not last. Within the week Dr. Street, the pediatrician down the block who'd nursed me through every childhood ailment known to medicine, had given me a statement reporting not only that my sleepwalking episodes had been few, brief and a long time ago but that they probably resulted from some summertime fever. Two teachers wrote similar notes; and so did my parents' doctor, who served, conveniently, on the draft board. By mid-August my case was complete and I was ordered to Camp Croft again. This time, shrewder and prepared to lie about anything that might threaten my acceptance, I sailed through the examination and, when I reached the same psychiatrist at the end, was passed with scarcely a glance. My affidavits seemed almost redundant.

The rest was mere procedure. Those accepted—now, to my relief, I was one of them—were directed double-time to another long frame building containing still more cubicles. The soldiers' perennial gripe throughout World War II, perhaps throughout all wars, was that we were always having to "hurry up and wait"; hustled first, we waited now—for clerks striped as PFCs and corporals to take their places at the wooden desks inside each cubicle, for our papers to arrive. When at last they did the line surged forward a few feet, then stopped again. We were given serial numbers and told to remember them. We were offered the chance to buy ten thousand dollars' worth of National Service Life Insurance, known universally as "GI insurance," which on my father's advice—he still had his from World War I—I did; the policy was issued then and there and handed me to take home, with the instruction that the premium would come out of my monthly pay. I was shaken to be asked whom the army should notify in the event of my death, a possibility I hadn't till then foreseen except as a technicolor drama devoid of blood or pain. "My mother, I guess," I said, lips suddenly quivering. "Better your old man," the PFC said, "this is no movie, Mac," bestowing on me for the first time the GI's term of address for everyone.

When the last serial number had been assigned, the last insurance policy issued, the last next of kin designated, the last paper clip attached to the last folder, we were herded off again, this time to the building through which we'd entered the induction center the afternoon before. The South Carolina sun bore down relentlessly. Outside the bus home idled noisily. "On your feet," somebody shouted, "and raise your right hand." As I did I recognized across the shoulder of the man ahead of me the familiar face of Purvis Ferree, a North Carolina golf pro whom I'd watched play an exhibition at the Forsyth Country Club in Winston-Salem and from whom I'd taken one brief, futile lesson. He was a bull of a man, with a red face and huge belly falling over the belt of his suntans, and his sleeves bore the two stripes of a corporal. "Repeat after me," he bellowed, and we all took the oath. I had ceased to exist as myself, as a citizen; I was ASN 34891454, and Purvis Ferree or any other son of a bitch with one stripe more than I had could have me killed if he wanted to. As we boarded the bus a crowd of recruits in dirty fatigues called from the back of a passing garbage truck, "You'll be sorrrry!"

iv

Like everyone else who served in the war, I said—and still say—that I was in the United States Army, but technically I was not. In order to meet the immense organizational needs of the sort of war modern technology had made inevitable, the War Department had created the "Army of the United States," a military umbrella, presumably temporary, that could accommodate not only the regular United States Army, which was small and voluntary, but the millions of wartime soldiers, like me, who were serving "for the duration plus six months," as in its conscription law Congress had decreed—without defining, perhaps deliberately, when the "duration" should be deemed to end and the final six months begin. This Army of the United

States made no difference in daily military life, when regular army officers and men were mixed with draftees without regard to their ultimate status, when whether a regiment, division or corps was permanent or only wartime did not matter. But the occasional regulars with whom one sometimes served, most of them old-timers looking to make the magic thirty years and a pension, never let us draftees forget it. They were rough and weathered, and though many of them were ignorant and indolent and never rose above corporal they believed themselves a superior breed of soldier; if dim on strategy they knew all the stratagems by which to bend army rules and customs to their own advantage. A recruit could do worse than watch them.

In September 1943, however, I knew none of this, and going home from Camp Croft for the obligatory "final furlough" my sole emotion was relief to be in the army at last. An eighteen-year-old of my fortunate birth and circumstance was unlikely to have "personal affairs" to "settle," of course, and I was so protected I would hardly have known what the words meant. But it was army procedure to give every inductee a chance to look after his family and finances before going onto active duty, and I had no choice but to take the furlough too. In reality I wasted the time. I'd lost so much already—first waiting to be called, then proving I was no threat to military security—that I was restless to go on in and start doing whatever it was I was going to do. I fidgeted, moped and was curt with my family and

Nancy and felt conspicuous to be still visible in anything but khaki or olive drab.

The time passed, however, and on September 24, carrying a toothbrush, razor and not much else, I boarded still another bus for South Carolina, this time for Fort Jackson, outside Columbia, where the army operated one of its largest reception centers in the South. It is an immemorial saying, beloved of American soldiers, that "there's the right way, the wrong way and the army way" to do everything, and, right, wrong or merely army, the War Department had developed a procedure for turning huge numbers of inductees into recruits, if not soldiers. The system was efficient, at least—for the army a rarity in itself—and reveals, in retrospect, a logic few recognized at the time.

The fundamental point was that it separated the process of indoctrination from, on one side, the process of selection and, on the other, the process of training: Camp Croft had picked which civilians should be inducted and Fort Jackson would turn them into recruits; it fell to some third place, still undesignated, to try to make soldiers of them. We were hardly off the bus before we were herded into a huge shed and issued our first, basic uniforms—two sets of khaki shirts, trousers, overseas caps and neckties; one o.d. (olive drab, the standard phrase for army woolens) blouse, pants, overseas cap; two sets of stiff green fatigues and caps smelling pungently of disinfectant; five pairs of o.d. undershirts, boxer shorts and socks; two o.d. blankets that were scratchy to the touch; two canvas barracks bags to carry them in; and, at the very end of the line, two pairs of GI shoes, heavy high-topped "clodhoppers" for which we were carefully measured and in which, before the issue was complete, we stood on a platform, loaded down with supplies, while a staff sergeant made a final check of their size and spread under all that weight. Like most city boys I hated them on sight, snobbishly associating their bulky ugliness with farmers and hillbillies; but the time was to come when I'd mutter silent thanks for their comfort and durability as well as the army's painstaking care to ensure their fit. An army may travel on its stomach but it walks on its feet.

I spent my first night as a real soldier in a real army barracks in a state of deepening embarrassment and acute discomfort. The long frame room, unfinished inside, with walls, studs and beams as bare as if they'd just come from the lumberyard, was lined on both sides of its center aisle with double-decker steel bunks. I had never slept in a room with thirty or forty other men, let alone in my underwear or—except at summer camp—without sheets on the bed. I itched all over from the coarse wool blankets above and beneath me, and, when the humid night heat made it worse and I threw back the top blanket, I became aware of how silly I must look in my skivvies. I need not have minded. The barracks hummed with the snores, groans, mumbles and farts of my fellow recruits, nearly all of whom, as I'd already realized, came from what later was called Appalachia and were as unconscious of their lost privacy as I was humiliated by mine. One of them, a gangly, white-faced redhead scarcely older than I, took out his false teeth and carefully set them on the windowsill behind his bunk. Others strode to the latrine at the rear wholly unembarrassed to be stark naked in front of half a platoon. Despite open windows the room reeked of sweat, dirty feet and intestinal gas. Silhouetted against the light from the latrine, one man solemnly masturbated.

This was not the army of fun-loving doughboys portrayed by the movies, and I was ready to get up next morning when, following a recorded reveille piped into barracks, a sergeant came through blowing his whistle and shaking the bunks of recruits still asleep. After a hasty but abundant breakfast—dry cereal, eaten out of the box, ham and scrambled eggs, mountains of fried potatoes, toast, coffee by the pitcherful—we were marched, utterly and hopelessly out of step, to another frame shed where medics awaited to give us our first shots, tetanus, typhoid, smallpox, diphtheria, probably the first many of the boys from the backwoods had ever had; several fainted at the prick of the needle. From there, already beginning to feel the shots, some of us feverish, we were led into what looked like an immense classroom, with wooden school desks in ranks and files the length of the long open space and a single bare table facing them. Here, we were told, we'd "take tests."

No one has ever explained to my satisfaction why the army made the single most significant determination of a recruit's military future at a time when—tired, still in shock at the strangeness of his new environment, frequently beginning to run a fever from his vaccinations—the recruit was likely to do his poorest; but I never met a soldier, then or later, who'd taken "the test" under encouraging conditions. "The test" was the Army General Classification Test, or AGCT, a modestly modified version of the hoary Stanford-Binet IQ test routinely and notoriously employed in World War I and in thousands of public school systems throughout the 1920s and 1930s. It was a measuring device bitterly assailed during the decades of its use: its critics repeatedly complained that it was heavily weighted in favor of the privileged, the literate and the educated—that it was "culturally biased," as critics of a later time would say of similar tests, arguing that decent homes and decent schools inevitably gave test-takers an invisible advantage and higher scores. The army blandly answered these charges by ignoring them: it needed some numerical measure by which to separate recruits into convenient lots, and it went on giving the AGCT, basing its most fundamental decisions about recruits' service on the results, till the war ended, as well as giving it routinely under difficult circumstances.

The test itself came, as best I remember it, in a thick, stapled pamphlet we were forbidden to open until the bell rang. Inside, arranged by such categories as verbal comprehension and skill, computation, solid geometric constructions and practical logic, were several hundred numbered questions framed for multiple-choice answers. Each category was preceded by examples. We would have an hour. No other instruction was offered. Pencils were distributed. The bell rang.

My immediate instinct—which was to save me again and again in the army—was to answer each question quickly and pass on to the next, never halting to fret an ambiguity or a dilemma. This turned out to be a lucky hunch, though no one had advised it or even warned me ahead of time that "the test" was coming and important. The pamphlet was stuffed. It must have contained nearly two hundred questions to be answered within the hour. The only way to finish, even approximately, was to hit and run. Faltering would be fatal. I did not reach that conclusion consciously; I had no experience to guide me, no big-city sophistication derived from years of standardized tests. I did it reflexively.

By the time the second bell had rung and the test pamphlets had been collected many of us were running fevers in earnest, sweating in the South Carolina heat and beginning to ache. But the morning's testing had only begun. Two different sorts of test followed: the first a series of mechanical diagrams and cross sections we were instructed to examine, then indicate, this too by multiple-choice, what action resulted in what direction; the second a sound test, based on dots and dashes, to determine how apt the test-taker was at learning signals. I worked quickly again, but with neither enthusiasm nor interest; I already knew my mechanical skill was negligible and I had no desire to be trained as a driver or grease monkey, let alone for the Signal Corps. I answered conscientiously: whenever I spotted an obvious error I made it.

The test done at last, we staggered off to lunch. The nearby mess hall was what the army called "regimental," meaning that its central kitchen was equipped and staffed to serve huge numbers of men through two chow lines on either side. I no longer remember what we ate from our divided aluminum trays, only that it was starchy and soggy and went poorly with our vaccinations. All soldiers in all wars and all centuries bitch eternally about their food, and their complaints are often cited, especially by those who do not have to eat the food, as perfect evidence of their robust mental health; but in fact—beginning then and there and with only a few noble exceptions—I found army food, whether served in large mess halls or small, overseen by master chefs or roughneck mess sergeants, ladled out by GI's who'd once worked in decent restaurants or by filthy cooks and bakers from deep stained pots in jungle mess halls, almost always terrible. Soldiers of World War II intended no witty irony when they named the hash or stew or leftover that became their most familiar delicacy "shit on a shingle."

Next day we completed the technical and bureaucratic procedures of army "reception." After breakfast we lined up to get long necklace chains holding our dog tags, a pair of identical brass plates an inch-and-a-half long by an inch wide bearing the soldier's name, serial number, blood type and religious affiliation, which was signified simply by an initial, "P" for Protestant, "C" for Catholic, "J" for Jewish—what a professing atheist or snake-worshiper was supposed to do was not indicated. By now it was clear that I had lost the middle name by which I'd been called, either in long form or short, since birth: to the army you had a first name, middle initial (or none, which made you an "NMI" on your papers and dog tags) and last name, so I was now James P. Davis, at least for the duration, and could like it or lump it. When I asked the dispensing corporal what the notch at one end of the dog tags was for he answered, deadpan, "To hold your mouth open when they have to identify your corpse by the teeth." I was not reassured by his saying "when," nor by his adding, unasked, "The extra dog tag's for your coffin."

From there we filed into yet another long open room whose rows of curtained cubicles were a sure sign of further interviews. These proved to be crucial, however, and again I was lucky, by chance drawing a bespectacled buck sergeant in his late twenties who seemed to know what he was doing, something few of the army's clerical personnel, I was eventually to realize, could claim. His job was to start my individual dossier, which would follow me throughout the war, by assuring that all of the essential facts about my birth, education, experience and aptitudes became part of my file. He had hardly begun when he looked up suddenly, eyed me for a moment and said, "Boy, you hit a home run yesterday."

"Come again?"

"On your AGCT, your IQ, the long test you took. You knocked it out of the ball park. You scored 131."

"But what does it mean?"

"It puts you in the top five percent of the army. Anything 130 or above. It makes you eligible for anything—schools, special training, OCS. You only have to have 110 to be an officer."

"So make me a general."

"There aren't any openings," he said dryly. "We're hoping you can wait till you're nineteen."

The interview proceeded. He listed my V.M.I. courses, asked what I'd like to do in the army if I had my pick—"besides commanding it, of course." I told him of my interest in chemistry, my basement laboratory, my summers working in the biochemistry lab at the Bowman Gray School of Medicine, my hope of pursuing a Ph.D. in chemistry after the war.

"Then we better try getting you into some kind of army science," he said.

"What about the Chemical Warfare Corps?"

He waved the thought aside. "They just make poison gas. It's idiot work. You want the medics."

V

At last I was, officially and recognizably, a soldier, a GI, or sort of. I had a serial number, a uniform, dog tags, ten thousand dollars' worth of life insurance and shots for every disease to which the army could foresee exposing me and against which modern medicine could protect me. I had a high IQ, a short haircut and the certain knowledge, mercilessly drummed into me by the "Mickey Mouse" film depicting the horrors of venereal disease, that my worst enemies, no matter where I went or whether I was fighting the Nazis or Japs, were syphilis and gonorrhea. All I lacked was assignment to some sort of training that would set me on the road to the Medal of Honor.

My interviewer had obligingly marked me down for medical training, and I had no objection to that, immediately fantasizing exploits paralleling the more romantic triumphs of Walter Reed; but until enough recruits could be assembled to make the quota required for a shipment to a medical training center I had to wait. Then and there began what would prove to be an extensive familiarity with army replacement depots—a fancy name for a holding pool of haphazardly qualified GI's awaiting orders to actual duty in actual outfits. The truth was, as before, that with its characteristic indifference to waste the army had inducted many more recruits than it was prepared to train or use but meanwhile must house and feed, a condition combining faulty planning and inefficient logistics that was to persist throughout the war and ever after. In short, the army knew it needed men but had no idea how many or where they were needed or what to do with them till it found out. Theoretically a soldier in a replacement depot was held till his specialty, or potential specialty, was sought somewhere; in fact he could be sent anywhere a warm body was requested. A good assignment took luck.

A replacement depot—"repple depple," to those trapped in one—could be spooky. Acquaintances occurred at random and rarely lasted long enough to grow into friendships. The soldier in the next bunk who seemed worth getting to know was gone next morning, no one knew where; sergeants with clipboards came through at odd moments day and night to rouse this GI or that for a shipment in half an hour. Rumors flew but were seldom confirmed: three guys down the aisle had gone to the 12th Armored Division; a fellow in the next barracks had been shipped to a cavalry center in Kansas; the whole barracks on the other side had left the night before for infantry basic at Fort Benning . . .

Days were long and empty. Once my classification was complete I was shipped across camp to a replacement depot in a north corner of the post, a dark warren of one-story tarpaper huts arranged in clusters of six around a latrine hut as functional and as rudimentary as they. A big mess hall, tarpaper too, stood at each of three of the four corners of the compound, a headquarters hut of similar design as the fourth, and it was through the latter that orders were processed and filled. No effort was made to disguise the impermanence of the place or its inhabitants, whom army lingo correctly called "casuals."

No one had anything to do but pass the day waiting. Casuals often pulled KP and now and then a crowd of hapless GI's were set to work on the garbage trucks serving all of Fort Jackson, but this was almost always a thing of chance, of being in the wrong place when the first sergeant came looking for bodies; and since no roster was kept for either KP or garbage duty the orderly room never knew who was working where. An observant recruit quickly learned not to loiter at certain spots, not to let himself become too easily recognized. It was unfair, of course, not to spread the army's most unpleasant chores around; but equity was rarely an important army consideration. Sergeants liked to tell grumbling soldiers, "It's hard but it's fair." A more truthful saying would have been, "It's hard, so keep out of sight." Street sense paid off.

But my luck held. I pulled a greasy two days of KP but learned from it where not to be caught doing nothing next time; I avoided the garbage detail altogether. Then, after nearly three weeks of waiting, uncertain and anxious, I was shaken awake before reveille one dark October dawn to find the first sergeant beside my bunk.

"Get your shit together and report to the orderly room at 1530," he said.

"To go where?"

"Camp Barkley, Texas. To the medics."

So, it turned out, were several hundred others from all over Fort Jackson, and they were an odd lot to see: limpers, overagers, fat men, more GI's with thick eyeglasses than I'd ever seen in one place, sleek boys near my age bearing Bibles and disapproving looks. I must have shown my surprise; the corporal who'd run me to the train said, without my asking, "Fucking dregs, I tell you."

"I don't get it."

"Limited service, most of 'em. Guys with handicaps. Guys with no teeth. Illiterate yokels. Guys too old to pull anything else. Fucking conchies—Quakers, Seventh-Day Adventists, shit like that."

I said protestingly, "I'm not like that."

"Better get used to it anyway," he said.

Every army post the size of Fort Jackson, and many smaller, boasted railroad spurs for bringing in troops and the huge amounts of supplies and materiel they required—and for carrying them out. Fort Jackson's ran, like most, alongside a row of sheds and warehouses with loading platforms; and it was from the latter that we filed, as our names were called by still another sergeant with a clipboard, onto the ancient Pullmans awaiting us behind an ancient engine puffing steam. It seemed to take hours.

The trip took days. Before finally coming home for good in 1946 I was to cross America twice by troop train and India once, but this crossing was my first and by all odds the worst. The fall was still hot in the rural Deep South through which we passed, the train innocent of air conditioning, the cinders through its open windows abundant, the stench of the accumulated sweat and smoke of several hundred unwashed soldiers, most from Appalachia and unaccustomed to modern hygiene, overpowering and the many long delays maddening. Moving troops may have been important in 1943 but moving civilians took priority, and our train spent many an hour idling on one country siding after another waiting for faster civilian trains to pass. Even when underway again at last it often moved so slowly soldiers, stiff, bored, restless, sometimes got out and ran between the tracks behind the rearmost car. The flat countryside—backwoods Georgia, Alabama, Mississippi, Louisiana, east Texas—was scrubby, bleak, hardscrabble, monotonous, pine forest following pine forest with only the occasional run-down tenant farm between, a collapsing cabin or two usually alongside dry, eroded cotton patches and small kitchen gardens going to seed in the harsh autumn glare. Now and then we stopped for an hour at some small-town station but were forbidden to leave the train for a Coke and Nabs on the platform. We slept in our skivvies two to a lower berth, one to an upper, and the stink deepened. Meals—boiled beef and potatoes, soggy fried chicken, endless gravy, endless string beans—came turn by turn, car by car, in an old diner located midway in the long line of Pullmans.

I no longer remember the places at which we stopped, though they were numerous, or the names and faces of my companions, though I still shudder at the stench inside the Pullman, to which I indisputably contributed. But the trip produced at least one figure whose presence has remained vivid. The train was under army command but was actually run by railway personnel, and among them were the Pullman porters, once part of the American legend. Ours, a huge black man of fifty-five or so, dressed in the customary spotless starched white coat and black trousers, liked to sit at one end of the car and talk with the young soldiers under his care. He'd worked many a troop train before ours and had, it seemed, a bottomless well of stories to tell about them, and not only about them but about the rails during the Depression years and about his time as a doughboy in France during World War I. He had a rich belly laugh and most of his tales provoked it, but he turned nearly solemn when it came to giving advice, with which he was also generous. He knew soldiering and he knew draftees were often unwilling to take it seriously; and one of his warnings struck me so forcibly I have had it on my mind ever since, because it reinforced a cardinal principle I had absorbed, whether I liked it or not, from the rigid daily discipline of V.M.I. "Listen hyeah, sonny," he said, poking a thick black finger into my chest. "The day you don't shine yo' shoes and don't shave yo' chin and don't smooth out yo' uniform the best you know how and don't clean yo' rifle and don't oil yo' rifle—well, suh, that's the day you ain't being a soldier no longer." He paused there, smiled so broadly his teeth flashed and—having milked his little drama for all it was worth—added, "Yeah, and it just might be the day you won't be living no longer neither." I have seldom heard wiser words. Eventually they saved my sanity. They may have saved my life.

A soldier's fate turns mostly on little things, some so small he is unaware of them, others in the past and so trivial he believed them insignificant at the time. I had friends who could hardly accept their luck in 1943 and early 1944, when the army, with more men on its hands than it knew what to do with, sent them to one or another of the ASTP programs at the nation's colleges and universities—only to be abruptly pulled out again in December 1944 and expressed to Belgium as infantry replacements, wholly untrained and unready, for the desperate fighting at the Bulge. I knew others whose minor gifts or skills—extreme good looks, a knack for guessing a man's clothing size at a glance, the ability to remember verbatim or type rapidly—landed them soft, safe berths as generals' aides, rear-echelon supply sergeants or headquarters clerks; and in every case the assignment occurred because the soldier was standing, as the platitude has it, in the right place at the right time. My own experience was that luck, good feet and discipline were essential. Luck is an imprecise idea no one can define; Americans are uncomfortable considering it but know they cannot control it. Good feet are mostly the result of genes, which are a form of luck too, and a soldier can only better them a little with towels, dry socks and talcum powder. But discipline is what he brings to war himself—discipline from within, not mere obedience to posted rules, which the army enforced far less rigidly than V.M.I. did or than its own more bellicose leaders pretended. That was what the old black Pullman porter told me as we chugged slowly westward through the heat and dust of east Texas; and it was to make a crucial difference in my life. Self-discipline: brush your teeth; wash your face; comb your hair; clean your shoes and shine them if you can; clean and oil your rifle. By such tiny details is a man's survival sometimes decided.

The landscape rose slightly, then flattened again into the unfamiliar tabletop plain approaching Dallas and Fort Worth, and as we plodded on into the night beyond them I began to feel the first pangs of homesickness. I was accustomed to the lush rolling country of western North Carolina, where a long line of mountains always marked the horizon, and to the even more dramatic peaks and ridges, the rich green forests and rocky mountain streams, of the Valley of Virginia; and the unbroken sameness of prairie and sage I saw in every direction was a more forcible reminder than anything the army could devise that I had left the infinite security of family and childhood behind. Others must have felt it too, for after days of boisterousness the car fell nearly silent—these were boys from the hills and dales of Appalachia, after all, for whom the mountains represented, as vividly as they did for me, the refuges of hearth and home and the safety, however primitive it might seem to me, they afforded. I had not expected this: I was a city boy, used to being apart from my parents and home and the comforts of the familiar; I had gone to summer camp for long periods since I was nine, had gone to New York with a pack of boys, had spent a year away at college; I was supposed to be immune to something as sissy as homesickness. But the hollow in my stomach only grew, and I skipped supper and stared into the night as we rolled on into the dark unknown: central Texas, a town called Abilene, an obscure army post named Camp Barkley.

vi

All army posts are more alike than different, whether they call themselves forts, camps, bases or reservations, and all basic training is essentially the same; but I did not know that in the fall of 1943 and had prepared myself instead for a unique, possibly heroic experience learning the arcane skills by which I would defend, possibly save, my country. Reality promptly replaced those innocent illusions.

We reached Camp Barkley in the deep darkness of an October night, backing in for what seemed to be miles to the long platforms alongside which were arrayed the canvas-topped o.d. trucks—the army's workhorse "six-by-sixes"—that in the next three years would become as familiar as Spam and boiled potatoes.

Beyond the lights of the siding we could see almost nothing, and we loaded up and drove off, in no discernible order, virtually in silence. When we stopped at last it was behind a row of two-story white frame barracks already so regular a feature of our lives we were too incurious to inspect them. We filed between them to a concrete company street where, as non-coms called our names from their inevitable clipboards, we shouldered our barracks bags again and stumbled sleepily into whichever barracks we'd been assigned. There we found double-decker bunks waiting, blankets folded at alternating heads and feet. We did not have to be told to quiet down.

That quiet was ended rudely and permanently before dawn the next morning by a whistle blast followed by a hoarse voice bellowing, "Drop your cocks and grab your socks! Everybody up!" We shuffled awake to see a wizened little man of thirty-three or -four standing at the head of the room with his short legs spread as he surveyed his utterly untrained recruits with utterly undisguised contempt. "On your feet!" he yelled, then blew his whistle again, a bad small boy, I thought, enjoying the havoc he'd raised. He wore a faded fatigue cap turned up in front, a faded blue-denim fatigue coat and faded green fatigue pants that ended in the most perfectly bleached—not whitened—leggings I'd ever seen; and, worst of all, he bore on his sleeves the three faded stripes of a buck sergeant.

It was a saying beloved by the cognoscenti in those days of fewer and slower promotions that "the sergeants run the army," and when I won my own three stripes later on I tried, despite abundant evidence to the contrary, to believe it; but what proved manifestly clear from the start was that all sergeants had immense power over anyone of lesser rank and that, of them all, buck sergeants were the fiercest. All were tough and most were able; harsh voices and rough manners were nearly universal, probably acquired at birth; and a remarkable knack for unsettling recruits from their usual indifference and complacency, and for keeping them unsettled at all hours, seemed to come to most of them as easily as breathing.

Sergeant Bruce Battee—as the wizened little man who'd whistled us up informed us he was named—was, and remains, the classic case. Like the rest of my training platoon I came at once simultaneously to adore, admire, fear and loathe him. He seemed beyond mere mortality: despite his bantam size and badly bowed legs he possessed the strength and stamina of a lion; he read recruits' minds, he knew "the book" from first page to last, whatever "the book" actually was, and went by it; he demanded the impossible, then showed by example that it was entirely possible; unlike V.M.I. upperclassmen he was hard but never cruel, for he aimed at making soldiers, not victims. He was clearly immortal.

He was also, that crisp October dawn, in charge of what we now learned was the second platoon, "C" Company, the 52nd Medical Training Battalion; and there, clumsily ranked and filed on the company street in front of barracks, we were brought by him to a slovenly attention, like the other three platoons of "C" Company and the other three companies of the 52nd M.T.B., while a recorded bugle call marked the raising of the American flag in the center of the hard bare parade ground that formed a dreary battalion courtyard. When it was over and the company commander had returned us to the sergeants, Battee gave us parade rest and delivered what would prove the first of his many sermons on military appearance, propriety and order.

"You are," he announced, his voice approximating the sound of gravel descending a tin chute, "the sorriest lot of stumblebum feather merchants it has ever been my evil misfortune to see. Look at you. Your shoulders slump. Your guts hang out. You can't get your feet together or your thumbs lined up against your trouser seams. You're disgusting and disreputable and I'm ashamed to have to be your platoon sergeant." He paused a moment to let his disapproval sink in, then said, "But I won't let you embarrass me. I won't let you ruin my army career. I'm going to work you so hard you'll pray to be delivered into the arms of Hitler or Tojo. I'm going to turn you into soldiers if it kills us both, and it probably will." All of this, delivered staccato, was terrifying and inspiring, a little touch of Harry at Agincourt, and I thought it remarkable, unique, as I thought Battee unique; and at that moment it was happening at every training camp in America.

"It" was basic training, which in the army's medical

department—contrary to popular usage the "Medical Corps" was confined to commissioned doctors—spanned seventeen carefully charted and measured weeks by which the army aimed to accomplish two sometimes conflicting things: on the one hand to convert raw recruits into soldiers competent in the fundamental physical and military skills of warfare, on the other to teach them the rudiments of public hygiene and emergency battlefield care. Again and again, however, the realities of the latter undermined the effectiveness of the former. An alarming proportion of the men assigned to the medics was, as my jaded corporal had observed at Fort Jackson, poor material from which to make soldiers. Men still of draft age but past the physical robustness of young manhood—some were more than forty—were numerous, and the demands of daily hikes under full field packs, let alone the even harsher ardors of the obstacle and infiltration courses, were simply too much for them. Many from the backwoods of Appalachia, though younger, were, through inadequate nutrition and childhood medical care, undeveloped, slack-limbed and weak. Still others were of borderline mental capacity and had trouble learning the most basic things necessary to survival in the field. Most of these were on what the army called "limited service"—i.e., they could not do combat—and so were the conscientious objectors, of whom we had a few, and the members of dissident religious sects, Seventh-Day Adventists most prominently, whose duties were circumscribed by religious scruples, practises and holidays. College boys were few—I was one of half a dozen in a battalion of a thousand—and so were men of my age, whatever their educational attainments, who were in good condition and intelligent enough to master the fundamentals. Around me on every side, in ranks, in the mess hall, even in the orderly room from which the company was commanded, the damage of the Depression showed in pale or lined faces, flabby bodies and understocked minds that could not be brought to concentration; and my privileged complacency was shocked to see it.

But again I was lucky. At eighteen I was one of the youngest soldiers in the battalion, and that alone, barring the nutritional and medical disadvantages from which so many around me suffered, almost guaranteed me a nearly painless basic training. To that edge my fortunate upbringing added another, that of solid early education, and my year at V.M.I. added three more: excellent physical condition, recent classwork in chemistry, math and English and—what suddenly proved of greater daily value than I could have predicted—an effortless proficiency in the most tedious requirements of elementary soldiering. I knew how to keep my uniform and person clean and neat, how to shine my shoes, how to load and carry a full field pack; I knew how to arrange my kit for inspection; but above all I knew close order drill. For none of these could I claim personal credit, of course. It was those long, hard hours on the V.M.I. parade ground that made the difference.

It was a big difference, and it was wholly practical. One night during the first or second week of training my platoon was marched to a dispensary a few blocks over, then left for a new round of shots. When we came out Battee had vanished. We waited, waited some more. Another platoon marched up and the area around the dispensary grew crowded. No one knew what to do: we were forbidden to wander back on our own. At last, no Battee in sight, I stepped into the street, gave the command to fall in, dressed the ranks and marched them back to "C" Company. I had no authority to do so and was as surprised to be counting cadence for a platoon of sixty as anyone in it—as surprised as Battee, for that matter. Summoned back to the orderly room while we were getting our shots, he was just emerging as, to his astonishment, his entire platoon marched up with me in charge. I turned them over to him and he dismissed them. Then he turned to me.

"Where the hell'd you learn to do that, kid?" he asked.

I told him.

"Yeah," he said, and took the tiny cigar from his mouth. He studied me for a moment. "Well, you saved my ass, and I thank you."

He did more. Though the platoon had a second lieutenant as its platoon leader and two shiftless corporals to help Battee, the overwhelming burden of our daily training regimen fell on him: all of them were married, had brought their wives to Texas and lived off the post, while he, though married too, had left his wife in Los Angeles and occupied a tiny room of his own at the front of barracks, a friar's cell of open studding as clean and as fastidiously kept as he was himself. It was he who was on the premises night and day, he who knew when his men got rowdy or sloppy, he who knew when a speck of dust fell or a sink grew dingy or a pair of shoes needed polish; and besides—as I think he would have said himself, but didn't—it was simply a platoon sergeant's *duty* to see that his men were prepared for the future, whatever it was, and to set them a soldierly example, which he did twenty-four hours a day. But he got little help from his corporals, who did no more than they had to and vanished, unless a night exercise was scheduled, at sundown. The demands on his time and energy—from conferences in the orderly room to commiserating with half-sick recruits who were lost and melancholy away from their familiar haunts and hollows along the Blue Ridge or Alleghanies—were endless; and to save himself where possible he began to turn much of the routine of formations and drill over to me. I knew how to fall the platoon in, as he'd seen, how to march them here and there in reasonable order; so, without quite telling me what he was doing, he'd say, "Fall 'em in, kid," or "Take 'em home, kid," and I would. I was his "gadget," he told the lieutenant, who was glad to let someone else do it; and, surprisingly, no one in the platoon complained or seemed to mind. I was able to spare them many a long wait, after all, and I had the gumption never to assume any larger authority over them. But it soon got me a cell of my own at the rear upstairs, a room originally reserved for the corporals, and Battee saw to it that my name was skipped for KP.

But he expected a lot of me in return. Besides being his "gadget" he meant for me to show initiative, to set an example in my own right, to lead when he could not, to grasp his meaning without explanation, to read his mind. None of this was ever precisely articulated, to be sure—as explicit as he could be in the field he was surprisingly indirect, even subtle, off it—and I only understood his method long afterward; but, still fresh from V.M.I. and full of its Virginia myth of martial glory, I reveled in my new soldierly duties. Though I certainly could not have said I loved the army, or that in the jargon of the day I'd "found a home" in it, I enjoyed the fantasy of being an unofficial non-com, a sort of sergeant, if only a substitute one, and began to fantasize further: that one day soon my brilliance would be noticed, I'd be picked for Officers Candidate School and in ninety more days I'd emerge a second lieutenant ready to command the invasion of Europe. Battee, whose formal education stopped at high school, and who as an unaffected member of the working class entertained no such hifalutin ambition, encouraged my nonsense. "Sure, kid," he'd say. "You can do it. You know the forks." He constantly, in the evening, asked me about V.M.I., which he knew mostly from Civil War lore and the movie *Brother Rat*, wanted to see pictures of it, picked my memory endlessly for details of dress and drill and custom. His rough exterior concealed another romantic, I suspect; and through him I glimpsed the chasm between American classes—where I took going to college wholly for granted he could scarcely have dreamed of it.

In the field, though, he remained a devil. He drove his charges—drove me—with a hardness only mitigated by his remarkable knack for knowing where to stop. If the platoon's close order drill improved he demanded further improvement. If it got better at hand-to-hand combat, as it did, he piled on and showed where we were still vulnerable—"puke-bellied sissies," he called us. If a man's field pack sagged Battee made him tighten it. But he taught as much by example as by exhortation. He cleaned and polished his own gear with the door open. He took the judo falls himself. He could outwalk a camel. He was first up and last down. He asked nothing he did not do too, and do better.

The men cursed but trusted him, for—though relentless and unsparing to the point, as many believed, of fanaticism—he was innocent of cruelty. He was a fluent and imaginative curser himself. "Goddamnit, Novakovich," he bellowed at a friend of mine one day, "You march like I fuck." I do not pretend to explain his drive or force. Except for a difference of eighteen months he was as much a civilian as we—he'd been a commercial artist for a newspaper before Pearl Harbor—but he brought to soldiering an aptitude and an energy few of the thirty-year regular army old-timers I encountered could match. Yet he professed to despise the army as deeply as most draftees did, and no more than any of us had he "found a home" in the drab barracks, barren parade ground and smelly mess hall where he now functioned so well. He was simply, I suspect, the sort of blue-collar man who was once the heart and soul of the American workplace: he gave the task assigned him, whether ad layouts or soldiering, the best his considerable intelligence could provide, and then some. It was not fanaticism, it was pride; and it won the war.

vii

Camp Barkley lay slightly above a dozen miles outside Abilene, a flat, dusty, wholly colorless as well as wholly uninteresting small city, or overgrown small town, that dominated that part of central Texas. Around it lay the cotton fields and cattle ranches that had made it busy and prosperous enough to become the principal railhead for shipping those commodities north, east and west during the last days of the nineteenth century—so busy, in fact, that eventually it eclipsed the importance, as it had already usurped the name, of the older, more famous railhead in Kansas. Its business during World War II was the soldiers of Camp Barkley, however, for their many thousands, including the more than twenty thousand men of the 12th Armored Division, had nowhere else to turn for recreation after a hard week of training and automatically flooded—as they were flooding similar communities all over the country, and especially across the Deep South and Southwest, where so many training camps were located—the movie houses, pool halls, bars, greasy spoons, whorehouses and occasionally even the churches of whatever town was closest. In Abilene, at least, some residents resented this tidal wave of lonely, rowdy and generally horny young manhood, and some showed it by placing signs on their lawns, the only ones I saw throughout the war, disagreeably and unpatriotically warning, "No dogs or soldiers."

This was unsettling, and few of the soldiers who took the army shuttle into town on Saturday night pass returned to camp with lasting affection for Abilene or its stuffy citizens, who were growing rich, after all, from the very customers they so openly despised. It was at best a dreary place where the overpriced food was bad and the natives unfriendly, the kind of prairie town whose main cultural event was the weekly ice-cream supper in the basement of one or another of the Baptist churches dotting the streets. Now and then one met girls there, but they were accomplished prudes, the daughters of barbers and insurance hustlers and Fuller Brush salesmen who viewed all soldiers, no doubt correctly, as threats to local virginity. The action was livelier, for those with the nerve, in the Mexican quarter, where there was an abundance of alcohol, even if it came as tequila, and the girls went upstairs for a five-spot. I lacked the nerve, alas, and in the end I lacked whatever it took to go to any more ice-cream suppers in pursuit of putative Baptist virgins.

It hardly mattered. Though Abilene extended me no warmer welcome than it gave most soldiers, we had little chance to visit it anyway. Regular cadremen like Battee and his corporals were free whenever not on specified duty, but trainees were always on duty except for Saturday nights and Sunday mornings, which we frequently lost as well. Besides, however, training was so exhausting we could do little more at night, even on weekends, than collapse onto our bunks after the daily grind was over, there to scribble drowsy letters home and, in my case, to scribble letters for my barracks mates unable to read or write, then fall asleep long before a recorded taps sounded at ten from the public-address system outside.

The daily regimen varied in its details as training progressed, but it always began with a recorded reveille at five-thirty, followed a few seconds later by Battee's infamous whistle. We fell out in T-shirts and fatigue pants for fifteen minutes of calisthenics on the parade ground, then went back inside and dressed in full fatigues for breakfast. Toothbrushing, washing and shaving had to be done quickly, a fact a few sluggards in barracks learned at a cruel price when they were savagely beaten in the latrine by faster, tougher recruits whose forced delays at the sink had got them penalized for falling into ranks late. Breakfast past, we formed again, in whatever dress was specified, for whatever class was scheduled for the first training hour: close-order drill, judo, gas mask practise, first aid, a hike under full field pack, map-reading, the obstacle course, the infiltration course.

The latter, easily the most terrifying experience basic training held, was designed to familiarize trainees with being under fire, especially machine-gun fire, and if possible to inure them to it. It was not possible, not to me or to anyone I knew then or afterward, to grow indifferent to the rattle and whine and the knowledge that real bullets were flying overhead; but it was the army's naive faith that if you shot at a soldier long enough he'd get used to it. The infiltration course at Camp Barkley fed trainees down a long trench, like those of World War I, that ended by taking a right-angle turn into another trench facing the guns; when the whistle blew the line scrambled "over the top" and began crawling directly toward them. The .50-calibre machine guns, which never ceased firing a sheet of bullets a foot or so above the ground, were anchored, stabilized and angled to maintain both a steady and a level field of fire—we had a safe margin, we were assured—and now and then a tracer showed that the margin was holding. But no one who was in it ever trusted the army to get things right, let alone to keep them right, and the terror was worsened for me by the dread knowledge, acquired at V.M.I., that the guns' vibrations made holding them to a fixed pattern almost impossible. I always ended the course with loose bladder and bowels as I reached the safety of the ground beneath the firing platform; but it taught me one thing—how to crawl. That was useful, but the more lasting legacy of the infiltration course was that I began to fear, and I was never able thereafter, feign bravado though I might, to free myself of it.

The obstacle course—an exercise in rapid individual movement across hazardous terrain—was merely demanding, and because of the conditioning I brought to it from the hard daily regimen of V.M.I. I had no difficulty mastering it almost at once. Camp Barkley's obstacle course probably duplicated others at every training camp in the country. Carrying full field pack, we were sent running, usually two by two, across a field littered with truck tires and broken by wide ditches filled with water, which we had to cross, sometimes by broad jump, sometimes by swinging hand-over-hand from a sequence of overhead pipes; at one point we crawled through a succession of culverts, at another, turned onto our backs, beneath a long platform only a foot or so above ground; and at the end, after crossing a pond by swinging ropes, like Tarzan, we had to scale a thirty-foot wall by rope as well, turning at the top to descend the other side by landing net. My youth and fitness assured me easy passage, but some of the older recruits, men in their late thirties or even past forty, were less lucky; I watched in horror as one fell from nearly halfway up, and more than one fell into the water or simply collapsed along the way. None suffered permanent injury, as far as I know, but all returned to barracks humiliated and hangdog, and I thought, and think still, that it was callous of the army to ask of them a physical prowess they no longer had.

More often than not the obstacle course came at the end of a hike, which—though precisely what was intended—did not make it easier. Marching was done by the whole company across the dust and grime of the Texas flatland beyond the camp gates, and the length and pace of the hike were steadily increased as the weeks passed. We always marched by a column-of-threes under steel helmets, which were not light, bearing full field packs, which were heavy. The business part of the pack contained a blanket, half of a shelter tent and one man's share of tent pegs, plus an entrenching tool—a short spade or short ax—these latter to be used to dig foxholes or a latrine or to fell small trees. All of this was secured by elaborate lacing and held to the back by suspender straps that hooked at the waist to an adjustable webbed equipment belt, which also bore a full canteen, a mess kit and two first-aid kits; and over the lot—pack, galluses, belt and field gear—we wore a gas-mask bag, fitting partly up under the left armpit, that was awkward and uncomfortable but had to be kept ready for use the instant, invariably unannounced, a gas drill was signaled by triangle. I no longer remember how much the entire kit weighed, but it was a wonder any of us could stand upright, let alone walk, once everything was in place; like the medieval knights in Olivier's *Henry V* we were ironically too burdened with fighting equipment to fight.

The trick was to strap it on tightly enough not to bounce but not so tightly that it irritated the skin or cut off the circulation, an axiom that might have proved good general advice for surviving basic training—for surviving the war itself. The regularity and order produced by discipline were not only desirable but essential; but obsessive discipline produced zealots, occasionally killers who thought nothing of the safety of others as they went mad in combat. Sooner or later everyone encountered them and usually turned as quickly as possible in the opposite direction, for though they were the soldiers who won the Medal of Honor or Silver Star they could be counted on to endanger the lives of their subordinates or companions, who if they survived at all won the Purple Heart instead. That, and not the overheated pursuit of battlefield glory, was what Battee's tidiness and dependability were there to teach us, I think: forethought, good habits, skill, *but not too much.* Measure was crucial.

One began to spot the madmen in basic training. I spotted one in a huge redhead named John from the mountains of east Tennessee who was so tall he stood in the rightmost position of the platoon's front rank, thus on my left when we fell in. He emanated physical power so completely, by body size, movement and voice, that he dominated everyone around him despite his near illiteracy; but he liked me and liked to have me serve as platoon guide when Battee was marching us, for my slightness meant I did not threaten him. I nearly always knew what to do next—my whispered hints spared him from making decisions he did not understand—and I wrote out his sentimental letters to his wife and parents in the lost, smoky hills he missed so terribly. Hearing Battee call me "Gadget" one day, he adopted the nickname himself, slapping my back so hard to show his good will he almost knocked me down. I liked him too, for he was free of malice and to any merely physical challenge he responded quickly and efficiently; but I would not have wanted to serve with him in the field. His rages were terrifying. He had the killer's red eye.

For my own part, which was that of a grain of sand in the Sahara, I was neither zealot nor goof-off. I knew it was practical in every imaginable way to do as well as possible as quietly as possible. As a matter of personal pride I wanted to maintain my self-respect in the face of the army's immense impersonality, and did. Above all—V.M.I. had taught me no more valuable lesson—I wanted to avoid trouble, especially the constant fist-fights and showdowns with non-coms, many on payday, in which soldiers like John seemed to wallow, perpetually bringing punishment on themselves and creating unnecessary disruption in barracks. I was no fanatic. I believed in American war aims, to the extent I knew and understood them, but I had little confidence in what the army was doing to achieve them, no illusions about its competence or efficiency. A few striking individuals like Battee apart, its leaders were dolts and its daily operations stupid, sluggish, hopelessly bureaucratic and dangerously automatic. Inertia reigned; rules, regulations and precedents were everything. But I was a realist. It would have been pointless, perhaps suicidal, to resist, even at the lowest personal level, pressures that were as inevitable as war itself. I had no desire, as young men of a later time would have, to "make a statement." In the army, as in politics, one had to go along to get along.

I could not close my eyes or mind to the idiocy I saw on every side, of course, but fatigue helped dull both perception and thought. The regimen grew tougher weekly, and, like everyone else, I was usually numb by the end of the day. Classes—most based on half-hour training films skillfully produced in Hollywood—showed how to identify combat wounds, how to apply the most elementary first aid, how to give morphine, how to bandage, how to move the wounded back to aid stations or field hospitals. We practised those tasks on each other; and one memorable day we were taught the fundamentals of bedmaking, bedpanning and bathing the bedridden in a mock hospital ward by Dr. Kildare himself, the movie star Lew Ayres, the most famous conscientious objector of World War II, by then a medical corporal and an instructor at Camp Barkley. We went through gas drill in a special compound. Two or three nights a week, sometimes oftener if someone in the platoon had blundered or talked back, we "GI-ed" the barracks, a bone-breaking task in which we literally scrubbed the barracks spotless with soap, brushes, brooms and mops, not to mention toothbrushes for the difficult places; windows were washed with Bon-Ami, the latrines with Clorox, and at the end we lined the floors with newspapers till time for inspection. Once or twice, dissatisfied with the result, the corporals made us start at the beginning and do it again.

To fuel the gruelling days of basic training we were provided an abundance of food no doubt high in calories but abysmally low in aroma, color and flavor, all of which the army apparently regarded as lacking military rigor. The worst of all the many hundreds of army meals I must eventually have eaten were those served at "C" Company.

Army mess halls inevitably came in a variety of sorts to fit the organizations they served. At Camp Barkley meals were served to trainees at "company mess," meaning that a single small mess hall fed a single small training company and no one else—the idea being that the presumed unity of basic training would be reinforced by joint dining. The four mess halls of the four companies that made up the 52nd Medical Training Battalion stood at the four corners of the big battalion square, each abutting its own company's four platoon barracks and orderly room. The mess sergeant and cooks and bakers, though part of the company, were hardly known to us except as we glimpsed them while passing down the chow line or at greater length, alas, while on KP. The chow line formed on the outside steps, in no particular order, and then passed inside down a single serving line separating the kitchen and dining areas; as a trainee turned from the serving line he was directed by the mess sergeant to the next seat at the next table. At this point his tray held only the main dish—eggs, meat, hash, Spam, rarely fish. The non-coms ate apart.

Each table seated eight, and on each—since company mess halls served meals, as the army put it, "family-style"—the butter, milk, bread, vegetables and fruit, cake or pie awaited in appropriate plates, dishes, pitchers and bowls to be taken individually; the servings had been carefully apportioned to guarantee an adequate amount per man, no more, and seconds were not offered. But neither the mess sergeant nor the non-coms made any effort to assure that helpings were fair, and I was shocked—protected by good manners as I was—to see the first soldiers seated serve themselves such heaping portions that little was left, often none, for those seated last. These "chowhounds" were not a majority, to be sure, and presently hungry soldiers like John cured them of their bad habits with harsh physical beatings behind barracks after dark, which may have been what the non-coms intended; but I missed most of many a meal till they did. It was my first real experience of human egotism, greed and indifference, I think, and it scalded me. "Family-style," perhaps, but not my family.

A miasmic stupidity resulting from widespread illiteracy and nearly universal ignorance set sharp limits in one direction on what basic training could accomplish;

the assumptions of the army about what a soldier needed to know set equally sharp limits in the other. Most of what we learned about battlefield trauma could have been learned in the boy scouts; it was hopelessly inadequate to what actually was needed in the combat of World War II, outdated in detail and only barely adaptable to the sophisticated combination of triage, penicillin, plasma and field surgery that eventually held American casualties far below those of the other major combatant nations. But even the rudimentary first aid we were taught was beyond the comprehension, let alone the mastery, of the majority of medical trainees, whose low intelligence and virtually retarded capacity for learning anything left them unfit, at best, for any but the most rote, menial tasks—in the words of the Camp Barkley saying, "The rest could be litter-bearers." Only in the realm of physical conditioning, ironically what I needed least, was basic training to any serious degree successful; and even there the deprivations of birth and the chances of upbringing had left disabilities that the best will and hardest effort could not overcome.

My own experience was different. I got along, did well; my strength grew and I learned easily what was there to be learned. I was bored, but the time passed. At Christmas, my first apart from the warmth and reassuring customs of home and childhood, my family unwittingly embarrassed me with a huge package of presents and food no one else in barracks (most of whom went giftless) could even remotely match. I shared around as best I could, but my plenty only emphasized their lack and made the day more miserable for everyone. Next morning, summoned to the orderly room, I was told to be ready for transfer before nightfall.

viii

My first thought was that somehow, after making so promising a start, I had blundered myself into a disaster even worse than basic training: the Christmas generosity of my parents and sister had aroused others' envy and wrath, perhaps, or perhaps some bureaucratic error was about to plunge me into outer darkness. No doubt this sounds paranoid, but *SNAFU*—to borrow the inelegant expression GI's used in recognition of the army's invariable inability to do anything right—was the rule. *Situation Normal, All Fucked Up.*

This anxiety at once proved both premature and unnecessary. Instead of being posted to the frontmost rifle platoon at Anzio I was being entered, the first sergeant told me, in medical technicians' school at El Paso; and there, after an overnight train ride across west Texas, I found myself next day. Officially the place was the William Beaumont General Hospital, a part of and adjacent to Fort Bliss, both of them venerable military posts named for heroes of the nation's Indian wars. At Beaumont, a large, handsome compound of stone buildings strung across a barren hillside typical in its volcanic aridity of the Southwest landscape, the army operated a School for Medical Department Technicians, to which, along with a couple dozen others from the various training battalions at Camp Barkley, I duly reported.

My orders had marked me for training as a medical or surgical technician—a slight step above orderly but below nurse—but at once that went by the board. Again I was lucky. The gray-haired Medical Corps lieutenant colonel screening my line of new students looked at my record for a moment, then up at me.

"You've had a year of college?" he asked. "Chemistry? Algebra?"

"Yes, sir."

"And worked summers in a medical-school laboratory?"

I nodded.

"Then you should go to laboratory school, son," he said, and with a stroke of his pen tossed me into the briarpatch. No degree of scheming or planning, especially army planning, could have produced so happy a result. I loved laboratory work, indeed wanted at that stage of my youth to be a scientist, but had I sought to bring it about I would have ended up doing guard duty in Alaska. Army logic occurred mostly, I was discovering, by chance.

Beaumont's school, which occupied the corner closest to the western edge of Fort Bliss, had six sections, of which the program for training lab technicians was considered the most difficult and most desirable. At the bottom level were the medical technicians, the "bedpan jockeys," who were slated to work on hospital wards; the section for surgical technicians prepared soldiers to assist in operating rooms; and those for X-ray, dental and pharmacy technicians, all three of which required a higher educational level, were meant to staff ancillary hospital services. Each had its own training facility, a double-decker frame barracks converted inside to its particular needs, but the several hundred soldiers in the school were housed willy-nilly in a cluster of green barracks at the foot of the compound. A single mess hall served all.

Lab section, the smallest and most selective, shared its training building with pharmacy section, its three big laboratories, plus offices for its instructors, occupying the upper floor. The first hurdle to clear was, in fact, the director of the program, Captain Frazier, whose mania for open windows had won him the universal nickname, "Fresh Air Frazier." He was a hulk of a man with immense shoulders and a neck like a bull, commissioned in the Sanitary Corps because he'd run a hospital lab in civilian life. He seemed to believe it his mission to turn lab section into an outpost of the

Rangers, for he sternly warned each man entering the program of his merciless intent to "wash out" any who fell below the strict Frazier standard—the first of many wartime officers I would encounter who used his uniform and rank to affect a toughness he'd probably never dared as a civilian. He pounced on me at once, as the youngest member of the new lab class, reminding me that my single year of college—everyone else had finished at least two and one had been a final-semester senior when the draft got him—made me, at best, a "probationer," as Frazier ominously put it, liable to summary expulsion, should I not measure up, at any time.

Frazier was a bully, but he had a point. From being the brightest boy on the block at Camp Barkley, I promptly realized that I had become the dumbest—or if not quite that the one who had to try the hardest. My IQ of 131, though extraordinarily high for the army as a whole, put me at the bottom of Beaumont's lab section, whose dozen members averaged above 140 and one of whom was virtually over the top at 165. Not only was my one year of college the lowest educational achievement of the class but the quality of my scientific preparation lagged far behind the others'. My high-school biology, chemistry and physics and my V.M.I. chemistry and algebra seemed like kid stuff alongside the advanced science and calculus they'd had at Northern high schools and colleges, where nearly all had taken qualitative analysis, organic and physical chemistry, biology, zoology and embryology, hardly known and little taught in the less ambitious institutions I knew. They'd attended—if not yet graduated from—places like C.C.N.Y., N.Y.U., Columbia, Western Reserve, Oberlin and Johns Hopkins, and their range and intellectual keenness showed in the speed with which they not only caught on in class but fitted new information into a rich context of knowledge and understanding already acquired. From the first day of instruction, and not just because of Frazier's threats, I knew I would have to hustle to keep up.

That was new to me, heretofore an academic front-runner, but exhilarating too for the challenge it offered. I found I liked having my mind and curiosity stretched. Most of my classmates, a couple of years older than I, were urban Jews, most, as their colleges suggested, from the cities of America's Northeast, Baltimore, Philadelphia, New York, Boston, and they bore themselves both in class and out with a sophistication and a worldliness that to me seemed almost exotic. They were on easy terms with things I had scarcely more than read about, subways, delicatessens, burlesque; knew music, theater; liked to eat in restaurants and promptly found the few good ones El Paso could boast; knew a variety of cuisines foreign to my bland Southern palate; could drink and not get drunk; could pass a free evening in town pleasantly and learn something in the process. They did not take the army seriously, let alone its pretensions or absurdities, regarding it as a chore to be completed, and my mastery of military minutiae did not impress them at all—they thought V.M.I. must be some sort of bad joke. Almost overnight, it seemed, I had been plucked from the near barbarism of Appalachian redneckery and plunged into a society in which intelligence, discrimination and taste mattered.

The work was as exciting as I'd expected but as difficult as I'd feared. As a schoolboy I'd never found it easy to memorize long accumulations of data nor done it well, and in the early weeks of the program that was a task to which, declining my classmates' invitations to go into town, I devoted several hours each weekday evening. But an added problem was the speed with which we had to move: the course was planned to accomplish in four months what ordinarily took the last two years of college; it could be done, like most wartime accelerations, but only by concentrating the material and by excluding such distractions as other courses. I, at least, had at first to run to stay even, to concentrate myself as determinedly as the army had concentrated the work. I was no grind, had never been a grind, and I liked to play; but the casual study of the past—an hour a day to prevent falling behind—was simply not enough to give me control of what seemed to me a daily crush of new information. I had to sweat to learn. That too was new, and I had it coming.

But it was work well worth doing. The smells of reagents, solvents, cleaning fluids and Bunsen burners were heady, and I loved handling the glassware—test tubes and petri dishes, beakers and flasks, pipettes and burettes, bottles and slides—the way a cabinetmaker must love walnut and mahogany. I was good with them, thanks to my summers in biochemistry, but less agile with such unfamiliar techniques as drawing blood or examining urine and feces. We learned on each other, with much obscenity and at some discomfort, all of us developing huge hematomas in the crooks of both arms as the weeks passed. It was not easy to puncture even a strong elbow vein on the first try, let alone a vein that rolled; sticking a fingertip and drawing a big bubble of blood to the surface was easier, though we soon discovered that the pain lasted longer.

The course was carefully designed to teach participants to perform all of the fundamental procedures employed by hospital laboratories at the time. The age in which much of this would be done by machines and computers was still far ahead, but technicians were still expected to do an immense variety of diagnostic laboratory tests, most of which, though that now seems in many respects still a horse-and-buggy period of medicine, provided essential information on the physiology and pathology of the sick and wounded. Time has broadened them and made them speedier to do, and many believe the results are more accurate, but it has not invalidated their central importance in differential diagnosis.

Instruction began with a month of chemistry, the longest time allocated any single area of lab work. We began with blood chemistry—hence our immediate initiation into the mysteries of venapuncture—covering the measurement of blood sugar and the more delicate assessment of glucose tolerance, blood urea nitrogen and blood gases. Considerable time was devoted to urinalysis, which was crucial to the diagnosis and management of kidney disease. Measurement of various bodily toxins was the overall task, and if we were not exposed directly to one or another of the rare tests we were told about them, familiarized with their general demands and expected to read them up in a comprehensive medical textbook.

Chemistry was followed by several weeks of hematology, in which, again with much blood-drawing, we learned to do red and white blood counts, a delicate business that proved to be one of the most frequent lab chores, then to stain and read "differentials," from which blood smears revealed basic data on the distribution and proportions of the various white cells as well as, sometimes, the condition of the reds. But my favorite among the specialties was bacteriology. I was still under the spell of *Microbe Hunters* and *Arrowsmith*, copies of which I carried in my barracks bag from post to post. The idea, then still relatively young, that many if not most diseases were caused by invading microorganisms, which might, once identified, be destroyed by vaccines or serums or specific chemicals, was as thrilling as a melodrama, and Paul de Kruif and Sinclair Lewis had heightened the romance. So had such movies as *Yellow Jack, The Story of Louis Pasteur* and *Dr. Ehrlich's Magic Bullet*, all of which portrayed the conquest of disease as heroic, even epic.

The fantasy that I too might prove heroic, even epic, in battling the great epidemics of World War II was farfetched for a boy of eighteen but not difficult to maintain in the bacteriology lab. Even more than other laboratories I found it and its techniques the perfect fuel for my overheated adolescent daydreams. Great emphasis was placed on ensuring an antiseptic working environment, so the Bunsen burners were always lit. Racks of sterile test tubes topped with balls of cotton awaited, as did stacks of sterile petri dishes filled with the violently red blood agar used for culturing throat smears. Boxes of shiny new slides stood alongside the microscope, which with its three objective lenses seemed infinitely more powerful than the child's home microscope with which I had examined onion skins and flies' wings as a boy; it was a leap into the dark unknown, where who knew what adventures lay, to stain a smear with Gram's dye, then flame the slide dry and clip it into place on the waiting stage, where a moment later the red and dark blue forms of bacilli, cocci and spirilla took shape against the bright white field cast by the brass lamp across the lab bench. We learned to identify the bacteria that caused diphtheria, pneumonia, anthrax and plague, and once, using the special technique the test required, we watched the pale spirochetes of syphilis slither sinuously down the darkened field. We learned how to cook a variety of culture media, how to brew cultures requiring heat to grow, how to clean used glassware, how to use the autoclave to sterilize equipment before its reuse. Not everyone loved bacteriology as much as I did, and some, fearing accidental infection, sighed with relief when we moved on to serology; but my fascination had only begun and would bear important fruit later in the war.

Boys are prone to imagining adventure and glory, but the pace of scientific progress encouraged it too. It was a time of enormous optimism about science and its possibilities, and especially about scientific medicine. Everyone possessing even a nodding acquaintance with chemistry and physics knew in general terms about the discoveries such European researchers as Bohr and Fermi had made only a few years earlier about the energy of the atom, though none of us at Beaumont could have guessed that their inquiries were nearing a demonic climax a few hundred miles north at Los Alamos. In medicine the development of the sulfa drugs had opened the door for the first time to fighting internal bodily infection with chemicals, and Fleming's discovery of penicillin had swung the door wide. Its successful broadspread use, a medical "miracle" in the jargon of the day, seemed to promise that the special plagues of war—wound infections, epidemics of typhus and pneumonia, vastly increased incidence of syphilis and gonorrhea—might at last be controlled and hundreds of thousands of lives saved. An era in which bacterial disease could be fought with confidence appeared to be at hand; surgery was moving from triumph to triumph, thanks to antibiotics and dramatic strides in anesthesia; and though progress in treating what was called "degenerative" disease—heart and kidney dysfunctions, stroke, diabetes, cancer, arthritis—lagged far behind, the advances registered against infection and trauma fostered and aroused a similar faith in inevitable scientific progress. Time and the intractable complexity of chronic disease would dim that faith, but in 1944 confidence was in the air. Even an ignorant and naive boy could catch it.

ix

After three months of dull Camp Barkley and duller Abilene it was heaven to be at Beaumont and El Paso. William Beaumont General Hospital had a professionalism one saw on every side, and its age and permanence, the solidity of its stone buildings and the orderliness of its daily operation were a reassuring reminder, after the cracker-box construction and incompetent boobery of Camp Barkley, that intelligence and stability still existed, even amid the disorder of a nation still trying to teach itself the ways of global war. It was exciting to attend class all day when the instruction was good and assumed its auditors had minds, and the conviction that one was simultaneously acquiring valuable knowledge and enduring skills was reinforced by turns in the hospital wards, where, as apprentice to Beaumont's regular lab staff, one could observe first-hand the way modern—and especially wartime—medicine was being practised.

El Paso provided a lively setting for all of this, and for those able to more fully exploit its many opportunities it provided more. It had an air of settlement that Abilene, in its cow-town tackiness, wholly lacked, the suggestion of a genuine local culture, with its fine business section and handsome neighborhoods, and it stood against its stark mountain backdrop like a fortress. What gave it distinction, however, was its unmistakable Spanish look and feeling. It lay at the westernmost tip of Texas where New Mexico and Mexico joined, and its southern border was in fact the American border as well, established by the Rio Grande, here little more than a shallow ditch but still a romantic name that seemed to echo the Southwest's turbulent nineteenth-century past. Fine adobe houses in the Spanish style lined the best streets; Spanish was spoken in stores and restaurants and hotel dining rooms. And visible across the river was Ciudad Juárez, simply Juárez to soldiers, then still a throwback to even earlier times, a "city" whose cafes, bars and dance halls had straw and sawdust on the floors, where liquor and women were sold on every street corner twenty-four hours a day, a perpetual invitation to GI's hungry for sin, sin a bit gaudier and more memorable than Puritan America encouraged, before saving civilization from the Nazis and the Japs.

These were impressions only, of course; I do not pretend that at eighteen I understood or could articulate them clearly. Moreover, at first I avoided the pleasures of El Paso—and the fleshpots of Juárez—altogether. Frazier's warnings had scared me, and the greater quickness of my classmates, combined with my anxiety, fostered in me an unfamiliar zeal to keep up with my class. But then things eased; I realized I was not as backward as Frazier suggested; and as my confidence returned I began to take advantage, as my friends already were doing with gusto, of the free evenings in El Paso.

The closest friend I'd made in lab school—as it developed, one of the closest of my life—was a New Yorker named Ira Singer, a couple of years older than I, who seemed to my innocent eyes the very embodiment of big-city sophistication. He was tall, slender, dark-haired, dark-skinned, with startling blue eyes which he used to great effect to convey his appreciation of life's ironies and to display his appetite and instinct for mastery. He was shrewd, knowing, what a later time would call "street-smart," and he came from Brooklyn's Flatbush, where he'd attended public school before entering college. But in his suave worldliness he was as unlike the movies' stereotypical gum-chewing Brooklynite as it was possible to be. Our friendship opened on an unpromising note. One morning the first week of class I asked him where he'd gone to college. "Johns Hopkins," he told me. "Oh, really," I said dismissively. "I hear that's not much of a school anymore." He made no reply, being of an extraordinarily mild temper, but he'd heard me; and then and there, he told me years later, he vowed to lure me to Hopkins—which, after the war, he did.

Having decided not to let my tactlessness interfere with a budding friendship, he began to urge me to come with him and others on their nightly jaunts into El Paso. I declined at first—though I was embarrassed to admit I was studying two or three hours each evening—but after a few weeks of acceptable grades, sometimes even good ones, I sighed with relief that I was not a dunce and relented. Ira had already—as eventually I would realize he did wherever he went—found the best watering holes and the choicest restaurants El Paso had to offer, among the latter the sumptuous dining room of the Paso del Norte, the city's premiere hotel; and he had determined not only what food they did well but, with his customary air of knowing best, what the rest of us must eat. None of us drank very much, I scarcely at all, but in keeping with the times I acquired a taste for martinis on those outings. Moreover, even if Ira knew best, the food was, with due respect to my mother's fine fare, the most delicious I'd ever put in my mouth.

As was often the case in that time of aspiration and fear, we made odd friends. Ira was New York Jew, I Southern WASP. He was subtle, patient, good at holding conflicting ideas and possibilities in balance; I was direct, blunt, sometimes inadvertently rude, always impatient, frustrated and enraged by inconsistency and uncertainty. I had in me a residue of the Confederate, a lingering idealization of soldiers and soldiering and the hierarchical system they symbolized, whereas he, though accepting the necessity of the war, saw the army as no better than a crude and generally absurd instrument for accomplishing its purposes. This made him, paradoxically, more tolerant of the army's innumerable stupidities, for he seemed to grasp what I still did not, that the world's imperfections were unlikely to vanish because of our brilliance and elevated intentions. He turned a forgiving eye to blunders, then moved on; I had a quick temper that made me contest every disagreement, every slight. His judgment was almost invariably good, and it made him easy to trust; mine was hasty and often wrong. He was bossy but never a bully; V.M.I. had made me a good follower, but I was so opinionated I could test others' reasonableness. We were very nearly a classic case of cool and hot.

Yet we hit it off at once and have continued to do so for most of fifty years. I have often wondered why. Apart from the fact that he was immensely intelligent and wise, especially at twenty, we had a mutual interest in science and medicine, and his ability to intuit the truth of a scientific puzzle always stimulated my imagination, which generally exceeded my actual knowledge; and to those qualities he added generosity and a calmness I instinctively knew I needed to acquire. Why he liked me is less clear. I was bright enough to keep up with him, but my boiling Southern disposition must have vexed him sorely. My hunch is that, for all my argumentativeness, he found me less boring, as well as far less predictable, than many others in our circle. I was doggedly loyal and dependable, but above all, I suspect, he found my energy—my spirit—a counterweight to his resigned, almost Oriental languor, for though his acceptance of muddle had not made him cynical it had left him convinced that, in the long run, little greatly mattered—so why bother? He led me, taught me; I spurred him, pushed him, and he often needed both. As with many friendships not only our strengths but our weaknesses were complementary.

Evenings in El Paso organized and directed by Ira were fun and broadening. So was—though hardly something I could write home about—a visit two others from lab class and I made to a Juárez brothel. Small boys, cabdrivers and full-time pimps solicited soldiers on every corner, so finding sex required no great ingenuity. But in the end, urged by three dark-eyed girls to "come fuck," we all lost our nerve and, the din of Mexican curses ringing in our ears, fled for the taxi, the bridge over the Rio Grande and the safety of the United States, Texas and El Paso in particular.

A social experience I could and did discuss with my parents had its origin in a common custom of World War II. It was a popular war, a people's war; people trusted each other, for their own husbands, sons and brothers were fighting it too, and they took each other in with a hospitality, and a lack of suspicion, that would seem foolhardy today. Giving Sunday dinner to a soldier was nearly universal, Abilene apart, and families were encouraged on every hand to do so. My mother, who by V-J Day must have fed every soldier at Fort Bragg, went further, writing a woman she knew from the Junior League that I was at Beaumont. Mrs. Anna Casten promptly wrote, inviting me to luncheon the next Sunday, with "cocktails at noon." I panicked at once. Cocktail parties were so rare in staid Winston-Salem that I had never been to one, nor—except for the odd martini under Ira's tutelage—had I done much drinking. I was terrified at my lack of sophistication. I called home, a rare occurrence, and asked what to do. My father was reassuring. "She'll have ginger ale, Cokes."

Alcohol proved to be the least of my embarrassments. Face washed, hair combed, I duly reported at Mrs. Casten's, a handsome Spanish hillside house on one of El Paso's most fashionable streets. She herself was beautiful and beautifully dressed, in her early forties, a woman of warm manner who quickly sensed my unease. Her husband was off commanding a battalion in Italy, she said. My spirits rose. In the living room they plummeted again. A crowd had gathered; everyone stood up; and as I was introduced I realized, soul turning to stone, that I was in officer country, and not only officer country but big-shot country—a brigadier general, a lieutenant commander, Captain This, Colonel That. "Call me Bill," they said one by one, "Call me Jack." I was a buck private, two or three months shy of nineteen, and my o.d. blouse was so bare of the insignia of rank or the decorations of valor I felt naked. I would rather have called God by His first name. I shuffled and stammered and was handed, at last, to a pretty teenaged girl obviously invited for my relief. I almost cried, all but fell into her arms. We accepted—my father was right—immense icy Cokes garnished with lemon. It was and still is the best "cocktail" of my life.

Girls were a constant preoccupation for most of us, whether Mexican whores or churchgoing teenagers, like the one I'd met at Mrs. Casten's; and because of Fort Bliss, an old post and a big one, El Paso was a soldiers' town richly populated with easy women, not all of them Mexican. Army "pro stations"—well-marked dispensaries to which soldiers were urged to report for disinfection and clinical prophylaxis promptly after sexual contact—were all over the downtown area, manned by low-level medics who stood on the sidewalk outside between patrons, one of the former being a West Virginia clod I recognized from basic training, a man both so uneducated and so stupid I could not help wondering how the army dared trust him with a responsibility even that routine. Most of my classmates in lab school were as innocent and as inhibited as I, however, and using a pro station would have been as unlikely for us as a walk on the moon. We were serious about our studies, moreover, and dinner, an occasional concert and a movie were the social life we mostly had. Even though we yearned for more lurid adventures the army's relentless drumbeat of warnings about the dangers of venereal disease, combined with the detailed acquaintance we were making with the horrors of syphilis and gonorrhea, kept us in a state of unbroken terror—and celibacy.

The demands of the course kept us occupied, in any case. After chemistry, hematology and bacteriology, which consumed more than half the four-month program, we were introduced, in turn, to serology, parasitology and pathology, after which we did a two-week residency, garbed in hospital whites, in the working laboratory of Beaumont proper. Serology, the least dramatic and to me the dullest section of the course, covered the flocculations, agglutinations and complement-fixations, the Kahns and Wassermanns, that were used to detect the presence in the bloodstream of a variety of antibodies and thus to detect infections often past symptoms or other kinds of physical or laboratory diagnosis. The tests required delicacy, patience and a practised eye, and they were crucially important to diagnosis; but doing them was, for me at least, dull, colorless work.

Parasitology, on the other hand, was fun again, taking us back to the microscopes and the recognition of odd, sometimes bizarre shapes, colors and movements. It was a first cousin of bacteriology—today they join with virology to form a single study, "microbiology"—but it dealt with larger organisms that, unlike bacteria, could not be cultured on artificial media. Our attention was focused on malaria, amoebic dysentery, hookworm, filariasis and the extraordinary variety of infections caused by trypanosomes, trichina and schistosoma; we were trained to make and stain smears, then to identify the exotic shapes on the lighted microscope stage—the agents responsible for devastating disease throughout the tropical world. In the South Pacific and on the Asian mainland American troops were suffering from some or several of them, often more cruelly than from Japanese bullets, and the threat they posed to our military operations there was serious. They were fascinating organisms to study, however rare on native soil, and the history of medicine abounded in dramatic tales of their ravages and partial conquest. I could not foresee, of course, that I would encounter several of them within the year, let alone that I would suffer from one of them before the war was over.

We spent less time on pathology, its skills being so special they could hardly be mastered within the narrow period of the laboratory course; but we learned to mount specimens, both fresh and frozen, and to make sections on the microtome, though not well. The microtome was a cutting instrument, akin to a meat-slicer though greatly more precise, by which extremely thin sections were cut, for staining and microscopic examination, from tissue samples sent over from morgue or surgery. The accuracy of the examination, which was done by a pathologist, depended on the thinness of the sections, which were prepared by a technician, so that a lot, sometimes a life, depended on the skill with which they were cut. All of us practised the procedure, but that part of the course ended with few ready to claim proficiency. We also learned to assist at autopsies, and on one occasion I was sent down to help dissect the tiny body of the two-year-old daughter of an officer at Fort Bliss. It was my first experience of the coarser realities of death, and it haunts me still. The conventional wisdom is that medical workers become hardened to such sights, but I never did.

My term at lab school was time well spent. I'd learned to enjoy the amenities of a city wholly different in climate, history, look and style from the one in which I'd grown up. I'd acquired a valuable skill—a "military occupational specialty," in army terms, "spec number" 858—that not only furthered my knowledge and understanding of medicine but seemed to all but guarantee me interesting future assignments. Beaumont's military demands were comically modest: an hour of close-order drill now and then, perfunctorily commanded and perfunctorily executed, a weekly barracks inspection usually even sloppier, a single night of guard duty. The food was adequate and there was no KP. We wore tidy o.d.s and neckties to class. Our instructors were professionals and, except for Fresh Air Frazier, intelligent and pleasant. As classmates we were convivial. Our evenings and weekends were free. Above all, however, I'd gained a belief in my own usefulness—so fundamental to a citizens' army—that basic training had failed woefully to inspire.

The only drawback was that it had to end; and it did, abruptly. No ceremony was scheduled. We simply finished. Frazier eyed me with his usual suspicion but offered his hand. No one, not even I, had "washed out," in his portentous phrase; and in fact everyone, even I, had averaged an A or high B. Orders came. A couple of class members went on to stateside hospitals; a couple more were assigned to hospitals already over-seas. But for the rest of us the news was dismal enough to deflate the good spirits our four months at Beaumont had aroused: back to Barkley.

X

Replacement depots, employed by most branches, were human warehouses in which trained soldiers were held until something could be found for them to do somewhere or other. The draft was efficient and dependable but produced a steady supply of more soldiers than the army actually needed or could use, the result being a chronic surplus of GI's with nothing to do. The army's solution, characteristically unimaginative, was not to put them to some constructive interim task but instead, simply to place them in some convenient place from which they could be drawn, like fish, as need opened new assignments. A replacement depot was known, appropriately, as a "pool"; soldiers sent to one were known with equal aptness as "casuals" whose status was "attached, unassigned," and their orders specified that they were there merely for "rations and quarters." All of this was army euphemism for inertia and boredom, for a replacement depot had no real function beyond feeding and housing immense lots of soldiers while they awaited assignment. But as the war wore on it acquired a more sinister reputation. Generals needing quick replacements often turned to whatever repple depple lay closest to hand, no matter what branch it represented; being a trained laboratory technician with a fancy "spec number" was no protection, if that happened, against waking up to find oneself, untrained and unprepared, in a rifle company. One heard such stories now and then.

The Medical Replacement Depot at Camp Barkley stood near a far corner of the post. To one side lay the Officers Candidate School of the Medical Administrative Corps, an invincibly tidy area populated by prigs so erect, spruce and militarily correct they compared favorably, details of uniform apart, with the staff of the first captain of the Corps of Cadets at V.M.I. To the other lay the German prisoner-of-war stockade, whose inhabitants, equally immaculate and ramrod, glared at us through the barbed wire. It was said that their food was better than ours, though that was no great achievement; and we could see that their barracks were tidier, more spacious and better ventilated than our noisome tarpaper huts. There we were, then: part of the army's

Lumpenproletariat of lost, unwanted souls, trapped with neither work to do nor future to envision between the glistening new brass of the Medical Administrative Corps and the clotted cream of the *Afrika Korps*.

No one had the slightest idea why we were there, or cared; and in that we were exactly like the thousand or more other medical replacements wandering aimlessly about the big bare parade ground—on which no parades were held—waiting to be told they'd *finally* received assignment. The non-coms running the orderly room answered all questions with bored shrugs; the two or three officers nominally in charge made brief daily appearances but seemed not to see us at all. Apart from a daily roll call we simply stood around smoking or sat around playing cards or walked around grumbling. Meanwhile the early summer sun grew brighter and the tarpaper huts hotter, and we began to envy the German POWs, who at least had something to do to help the time pass; and because they did their backs and chests were brown, their flaxen hair gleamed in the bright light, their muscles rippled. They ran Camp Barkley's garbage trucks.

Presently—though it was hardly what we'd hoped for—we found employment. One June night just before taps the first sergeant strode into the hut, accompanied by the mess sergeant, who appraised us like cattle. "They'll do," he said at last, whereupon the topkick said, "You guys go on KP at 4:30 tomorrow, and I don't mean P.M." "How long?" one of us asked. "Till I tell you different, wise guy," the first sergeant said.

Groans filled the darkness that followed, and when the inevitable whistle blew before dawn they had grown despairing.

There was much to despair of. We were not fighting at Monte Cassino, to be sure, nor were we stagnating in some English port awaiting orders to embark for Omaha Beach; but they were far away, as everyone else's combat always is, and the mess hall serving the replacement depot at Camp Barkley was only a hundred feet distant. A strange, wan creature whom I remembered from basic training—one of the Appalachian illiterates who, despite the army's best efforts, still could not read and write, probably retarded (in the words of a later time), certainly feebleminded (in the words of that one)—was our "KP pusher"; and he aroused our instant hatred by chanting loudly, even when it should have been obvious that his whistle had done the trick, "Everybody up, everybody up, everybody up," again and again, in a singsong way that made it clear that we were in the hands, for God knew how long, of one of the army's most dogged dimwits. But he was in charge, the mess sergeant's man, and we had no option, till we'd spied out the territory, but to do as he said; so off we went to the mess hall, already a steam bath in the humid early morning.

It was what the army called a "regimental" mess hall: a big central kitchen serving long cafeteria lines on either side, able to feed a thousand men at a meal, more in a pinch. Huge pantry rooms stood adjacent to the kitchen, and long walk-in refrigerators and freezers, and another room held extra crockery and stainless-steel utensils and serving trays; and at either corner of the kitchen proper, the horror haunting KP's everywhere, stood the washroom, open to the eating area, through whose portals dirty trays and knives and forks were pushed for scraping, disinfecting and washing and drying. *Its* corner, the ultimate horror, belonged to the huge washtubs reserved for whichever luckless clucks drew "pots and pans."

Murray Aronson, a friend from lab school, and I were the luckless clucks, and I knew at once that the good fortune I'd enjoyed since entering the army, and begun taking for granted, was over, probably forever. Bathed in steam, we were set to work on huge greasy pots somehow left unwashed from the night before, the residue of inedible, unthinkable foods having hardened in the interim; and we were still midway through that when the breakfast cooking pots began to arrive from the kitchen. They kept on coming, and the pressure rose further when the mess hall opened, serving began and foul eating trays started coming through, the dirtiest and most difficult being passed on automatically to us. Murray, a New Yorker with an excellent mind and a couple of years at Columbia, was so short he could barely extend his arms across the sinktop and into the hot water, but the glitter in his eyes told me he was already calculating means of escape; and at one point—evidently having persuaded himself that as a Southerner I must be adept at such rude domestic tasks, which of course no resident of Central Park

South would dream of tackling—he turned from the sink and with a benign little smile said, "I suppose you're accustomed to this." "No, Murray," I said. "We have Yankee overseers to make sure the slaves do it for us."

Our buddies were faring only marginally better. Ira Singer had insinuated himself into what appeared to be a soft spot on the serving line, but by the end of the day—hassled by an émigré German mess officer who repeatedly warned him that "Mustard must be mit a dash"—he confessed himself broken in spirit, and with a sore forearm to boot. Others found themselves endlessly sponging off tabletops and mopping floors, while still others spent the day on the delivery-ramp steps peeling an uninterrupted procession of Irish potatoes. The heat of the building, past one hundred degrees by breakfast, grew murderous.

This could not last, but it did. KP ordinarily came a day at a time and was rotated among the available victims; unless you found an out you took your turn. Ours was not by turn but by fiat, and it lasted three days, four, one week, two. This was a violation of all rules of fairness, of common decency, probably a violation of the Articles of War, the Geneva Convention and the Four Freedoms. KP for *us*? The *cream* of the army? At last the glittering little eyes of Murray Aronson provided evidence that a scheming little brain lay behind them. He was assisted in this heroic work by Ira Singer, and their plot was promptly entitled *The Aronson-Singer Caper*. Like all great creations it rested upon an indisputable reality and built upon its logic. No one in charge had the faintest idea in which of close to fifty huts any of the more than one thousand men in the replacement depot actually lived, Murray solemnly reminded us: when they wanted someone by name they summoned him to the orderly room through the public-address system. Nor did the mess sergeant know our names, while the KP pusher was too stupid to remember them. Thus the solution to our problem, Ira now chimed in, was to watch for a night when a large shipment of men left a number of cots empty elsewhere, then pack, move out in the darkness and find new cots in new huts, leaving the present ones empty when Pusher arrived before reveille. The mess sergeant would be furious, but what could he do but find a new lot?

"Yeah, but suppose one of us lands in the hut he comes to next?" someone asked.

"Fortunes of war," Ira said with Flatbush worldliness. "Think of it as a prison break."

Our chance came the next night. Forty men or more had been seen boarding trucks that morning, barracks bags and all, bound for new assignments. After taps we readied ourselves. Possessions were assembled, bags filled. The compound fell silent. We shouldered bags and started for the door. Then the unforeseen happened. The screen creaked open. The lights clicked on. Pusher strode in. His eyes blinked behind his thick glasses, but even he saw at a glance what we were doing. "What the—" he began, but his question went unfinished. No signal had to be passed. The two men nearest him threw him to the floor. The rest of us surged forward and piled on, pummeling him with our mess kits until his groans ceased. Someone cut the lights. We fled like wild birds, neither knowing nor much caring whether we'd merely downed Pusher or killed him. We deserved reproach; but Pusher didn't die, at least at our hands. Someone sighted him in the mess hall next day, harassing a new crew of KP's and looking little the worse for his ordeal apart from a conspicuous shiner around his Coke-bottle spectacles. As for us, our escape was a rarely successful switch on the army. We found cots all over. For a few days, avoiding recognition, we ate surreptitiously at neighboring mess halls, then wandered back, one by one, into our own. None of us was ever spotted or caught, let alone punished, though Ira was convinced that the émigré German mess officer—"mustard mit a dash"—eyed him suspiciously one morning as he passed down the serving line.

Putting one over was heady; but repple depple went on, and as our term in limbo lengthened we drifted here and there. At one point, for no discernible reason, a group of us were sent into the scrubby Texas countryside to finish out a two-week bivouac with a training battalion, returning by a twenty-five-mile forced march with great masses of foot blisters to show for the experience. We got new shots, though our old ones were up-to-date. We had our teeth checked. I read a lot of books and all of us saw a lot of movies, which were cheap and changed often. For a couple of weeks

Ira and I worked—cushy jobs—in the Camp Barkley art department, which produced silk-screen posters, training displays and signs for outfits all over the post. For one glorious week I was launched on track for OCS, sitting for interviews, writing examinations and appearing before one board after another, from which I drew the flattering inference that I would yet end a major general—until reality returned at the final board and I was rejected for a lack of "command presence." I had just turned a gawky, immature nineteen, old photographs make clear; but I was deeply surprised to be denied, at the very least, a regiment of my own.

Few features of war are more universal, or more certain, than boredom; its occasional episodes of excitement or danger may conceal, but they cannot dispel, the daily tedium in which most soldiers mostly live while they wait, and wait, and wait. Prolonged boredom, itself enervating, in turn produces another evil: in the soldier himself it engenders a deepening sense of his own uselessness; he becomes flabby physically, morally; his skills, whether for bayonet or test tube, begin to wither. In a purportedly democratic army fighting a war purportedly waged on everyone's behalf, the conviction that one is playing one's part is crucial, a decline in morale destructive. That was what Camp Barkley's replacement depot very nearly did to us. It was not, in the end, the exhaustion of KP, the senselessness of another bivouac, the stupidity of vaccination when one's record showed new vaccination was unnecessary; it was the sinking certainty, never precisely articulated, that our training, our spirit and ultimately ourselves were being wasted.

The weeks dragged on; Texas broiled in the cruel sun of June, July, early August; and still nothing happened. Then without warning, as always seemed the army way, Ira and I were told to pack.

xi

The immediate move was only across camp, but the omens were promising.

By World War II American military medicine had reached a high level of sophistication and organization. Stateside camps and bases and rear-echelon areas overseas offered dispensaries, clinics and post hospitals within the easy reach of almost any sick or injured soldier. In the field an entire pyramid of medical institutions replaced the dreaded "butchers' shops" of earlier wartime infamy: "aid stations" for front-line triage and emergency surgery, "evacuation," "field" and "mobile surgical" hospitals (the latter the forerunners of the M*A*S*H units of subsequent celebrity) for intermediate care, with "general" hospitals, large, medically comprehensive and more or less stably located, to support them all. In the United States itself a sturdy array of big, permanent general hospitals, many specializing in long-term care in amputation, orthopedics, thoracic wounds, neurosurgery and psychiatric disorders, assured the seriously wounded or sick the most advanced professional medicine then available: Brooke General in San Antonio, Letterman General in San Francisco, Fitzsimmons General in Denver, Beaumont General in El Paso and others. And at the head of the whole system, the command post for all army medicine, stood Walter Reed Hospital in Washington, impressive and reassuring in its solidity and established reputation.

The assignment Ira Singer and I suddenly drew in early August was to something called the 172nd General Hospital, till then unknown to either of us; but since it was located across Barkley, which had a post hospital of its own and was not entitled to a "general" hospital anyway, we knew at once, even before reaching its orderly room, that we must be joining a newly created outfit and thus, better still, must soon leave Camp Barkley, Abilene and even, if God answered prayer, Texas itself.

First Sergeant Bill Terry, a strapping six-footer in his late twenties, checked us in against a list on the inevitable clipboard, then pointed down two parallel rows of tarpaper huts dismayingly like the ones we'd just left. "Bunk anywhere you can find space," he told us.

"We're not going to be here long anyhow." As if in afterthought he added, "Look smart, you guys. We're going to be passing out stripes one of these days."

By now, what with this ordeal and that, I'd become what I considered a seasoned soldier—or at least a seasoned "garrison" soldier, as they said—and knew my way around: I could drill as well as any marine alive, sail through any inspection invented, master any obstacle course or survive any infiltration course I'd met, outwit any company clerk who hassled me, finagle any pass I really wanted, avoid fighting and please platoon leaders, first sergeants and company commanders. These were the "street smarts" of the GI's trade, so to speak, the visible evidence of his proficiency, and—good little ex-V.M.I. cadet I still was—I was proud of them. Unfortunately for my martial pride, however, they had little or nothing to do with my new assignment. Bill Terry and a few others amongst the handful of non-coms brought in to get things started might appreciate my snappy way with a uniform and my parade-ground bearing for five or ten seconds; but no one else noticed or cared. This was a *hospital*, I saw, not an ROTC summer camp, and in it medical knowledge and skill would be what mattered.

I was, as always, in need of the reminder. A part of me, pursuing the Lost Cause to the last, still clung to the threadbare romanticism of arms and glory. But I quickly caught on. My hut, already almost full, included a middle-aged chiropractor, an optometrist, an operating-room attendant from the Mayo Clinic and a tall, weathered fellow with dusty spectacles and a Ph.D. in paleontology, all of them draftees, all of them privates and all of them immeasurably more experienced, personally and professionally, than I was likely to become before the end of the twentieth century. They shuffled through our occasional formations with an awkward indifference I found shocking; worse yet, no one, not even First Sergeant Bill Terry, uttered so much as a syllable of correction or reproach. V.M.I.'s importance began to undergo an overdue reduction.

Organization proceeded, and as it did the whole pace of army life, so turgid and purposeless only days before, seemed to quicken. Every day brought fresh truckloads of newly assigned enlisted men. Sections took shape: Ira and I were two of the dozen lab men; others drew spots, as their spec numbers disposed, to the operating room, dental clinic, X-ray, pharmacy and wards, while still others, unprepared for any specialty, formed the hospital's large maintenance and service crew; a sizable number, trained as clerks and typists, were assigned to hospital headquarters to keep records and manage day-to-day activities, and the kitchens, of which eventually there would be several, got the men trained, somewhere between basic training and now, in one or another of the army's many cooks-and-bakers schools. Bill Terry, a first sergeant who actually worked at his job, held military nonsense to a minimum and concentrated on the complexities of putting a unit of two hundred and fifty enlisted men together, organizationally and administratively, as promptly and as efficiently as possible. He had to sort us out; a successful fusion of our various skills, talents and personalities, which would determine our ultimate worth, would have to come when and if it came.

Our professional officers—our internists, surgeons, urologists, gastroenterologists, radiologists, pathologists, bacteriologists and dentist—would join us at our next stop, he told us.

We'd get our nurses still later.

Presently, though he did not say when or where, we would undertake "parallel" training—i.e., for a month or so we'd work side by side with our counterparts at a permanent stateside general hospital.

Whereafter, he said, we were going overseas . . .

No, never mind where. A slip of the lip, remember.

But first and next—here he paused for maximum effect—we could all go home on furlough.

By that time most of us were on the brink of madness from being in Texas too long—I had been there nearly a year—and the prospect of furlough produced tumultuous cheers. Like almost everyone else I scrambled at once into Abilene to wire home for money; but cash was a minor problem. The larger one was that Camp Barkley was not only figuratively but literally nowhere: train and bus routes were local and required so many changes before one reached an efficient cross-country connection that anyone living east of the Mississippi faced a formidable task. Nothing would do, a group of us finally agreed, but to hire a hack to Dallas, where, timetables told us, we could at least find frequent trains pointed home. Even that proved, under wartime gasoline rationing, easier to plan than do; but at last, grossly overcharged even for Texas, we set off, parting in Dallas—after a long night on the grass in front of the train station necessitated by a shortage of hotel rooms and the indisputable fact that we were grubby enlisted men, not officers—to take whatever connections we could find. Mine proved terrible but typical of World War II travel: east to Memphis, where I had to change not only trains but stations and nearly missed my car; south through Mississippi aboard the decrepit Frisco line, windows open to a relentless hail of cinders and soot; northeast to Atlanta and from it north to Greensboro, where I finally got a Greyhound bus the last thirty miles to Winston-Salem; and a Blue Bird taxi home. I arrived at four in the morning, awakening my parents with a volley of gravel on their bedroom window, after traveling sixty hours and standing up the entire time. No wonder nations make boys fight their wars.

I was overjoyed to be home and would gladly have remained there forever; but I botched the furlough. I wasted no time on sleep but would've been wiser if I had. Youth notwithstanding, I was exhausted from the long trip and the longer period of suspension before it, and the exhaustion made me testy. I was sulky with my parents, whom I accused of colluding, like all civilians, in the army's innumerable insanities, and swaggered in the presence of my friends' parents, the Southerns and the Speases, to whom I was almost as close as I was to my own. I was cross with Nancy, whom I loved with the hopelessness of a puppy, and ended by provoking a quarrel. The truth, I believe I knew even then, was not my bluster, however; it was that I was simply scared. I dreaded the two-day return trip, which with the two days I'd taken getting home reduced my furlough from twelve days to eight. I dreaded the uncertainties of the coming weeks and months. But above all I dreaded "going overseas," which with its secrecy and unforeseeable fortunes could mean almost anything and anywhere and seemed to me, as it did to almost every soldier of that time, a plunge into the fearsome void.

It was an age of profound emotional innocence: America's war was, by its endlessly repeated assertion, a "good" war, a "just" war, a "crusade" against the undeniable evils of Hitlerism and Tojoism, and neither American society nor the dominant habits of American masculinity encouraged or provided the means of confessing fundamental doubts or anxieties, let alone of admitting to fears that later generations would regard as natural and inevitable. I suffered them in the same silence into which all the young men of my age descended—or rather in a cranky exhibition of bravado that was the opposite of what I really felt—and returned to Camp Barkley and the 172nd General Hospital in a kind of bewildered relief. The paradox was troubling but beyond me to resolve: I loathed the army but welcomed its familiarity; I found the civilian world to which I longed to return alien and incomprehensible.

Back at camp the bustle of organizing a new outfit made the army itself comprehensible for the first time. Confusion and error were abundant as we shook down, but the realization that at last we had a purpose and that the chaos was only the temporary preliminary to doing the work we'd been trained for proved exhilarating. The direction of Bill Terry and the other senior sergeants brought order quickly. We were not yet a functioning hospital, of course—we had neither doctors nor nurses, neither buildings nor equipment—but sections were established, each the skeleton on which the great variety of duties performed by a general hospital would be hung; and within each, at daily sessions conducted mostly on the hard Texas ground, the work was subdivided and tasks assigned. Laboratory section, a dozen enlisted men still without a pathologist, a hematologist or a bacteriologist, was led in the interim by a staff sergeant who'd come from Brooke General Hospital at Fort Sam Houston; he was in charge but, recognizing at once that his new lab, like most, was a rich assortment of prima donnas who knew not only what they were doing but what they did best and what, in particular, they wanted to do, wisely let his underlings sort out things for themselves. Tom DeGraffenried, a volatile fellow in his late twenties who'd taught high-school science before receiving Uncle Sam's greetings, took on the chemistry section. Miles Conrad, the tall, owlish Ph.D. in paleontology, went in with him, there being no call for the excavation and study of fossils; and Dick Towey, forty, florid and a veteran of the

Mayo Clinic who knew more about the ways of hospitals than most of us would ever learn, took on the delicate work of pathology, though he had a fondness for spirits and sometimes turned up in the morning with shaking hands that worried everyone who foresaw him handling the microtome blade, a cutting edge sharper by far than a straight-edged razor. Others took seats where their training indicated or where they were needed. Ira and I loudly requested and—since no one else wanted it anyway—got bacteriology. Harmony reigned.

Harmony remained, too, or at least in lab section as long as I was a member of the 172nd General Hospital. This was not true throughout the unit, which as time passed revealed that it was rich in the number and diversity of its staff's interests and ambitions. Few hospitals, civilian or military, do more than barely conceal their jealousies and rivalries, and large general hospitals proved throughout the war to be especially fertile in fostering professional resentments that inevitably passed on to the enlisted men. The 172nd was no exception, if the stories I heard after leaving it, and after the war, were true; but during the many months I belonged to it serious intrigue did not reveal itself—perhaps, despite difficulties of a sort that would be expected to foster trouble, because for a long time the full staff was still not assembled and the full range of its work still had not begun. Doctors are a fractious lot, and to that professional characteristic the army's hierarchy of ranks and privileges added sinister complications. But that happened, to whatever extent it happened, after I had transferred elsewhere.

Amongst us in the laboratory, at any rate, a good spirit of cooperation and mutual respect prevailed. Most of us were highly pleased to be there and gratified at the prospect of interesting work in subjects we already knew we liked. Most of us liked most of the rest, which helped, and were wise enough to mute differences. Miles Conrad, who seemed to me ripe with the experience of great age—he was thirty-three—entertained no military ambition whatever; he would have been happy to remain a buck private forever and longed only, it appeared, to return to his wife and children in Tarrytown, New York, and his job at the American Museum of Natural History, for which only a few years before he had gone on an expedition to the Gobi Desert. Dick Towey may have been a drinker but he was a charming companion who told endless stories about the sexual shenanigans of celebrities hospitalized at the Mayo Clinic. Ira and I were congenial not only as friends but as co-workers; our mutual interest in bacteriology, though it still lacked the learning of the old, had the enthusiasm of the young.

We talked; we waited; and then Bill Terry assembled us for the expected announcement. Two days later we were on a troop train bound for Utah, where we'd go "parallel" with Bushnell General Hospital at Brigham City.

xii

Most of us would happily have razed Texas and spread salt on the rubble, but leaving it would serve. After a year of it we'd nearly forgotten that a temperate climate and tolerable people could exist, and the prospect of even a brief time in Utah, though in fact we knew next to nothing about Utah, was sweet.

The reality proved even sweeter. Winding its way north through the Rockies, whose waters, colors and dramatic heights quickly erased the sagebrush monotony of central Texas, the troop train passed through Denver and Salt Lake City and deposited us on a siding at Bushnell General Hospital, from which we were driven a quarter of a mile to a cluster of frame barracks in one corner of the hospital compound. Mountains already accented with early snow framed the horizon in every direction; the air was fragrant, the sky pellucid; and between our separate huts peach trees heavy with the fruit of a chilly autumn stood only inches from easy picking.

This was promising beyond our rosiest hopes, and Brigham City, whose limits lay just past the main gate of the hospital, promptly fulfilled them too. Its name notwithstanding, it was a classic small town, handsomely laid out by pioneer Mormons a century or so earlier along the gentle slopes of Box Elder Canyon, serving as a processing and shipping depot for the abundant produce grown in northern Utah. It was as pretty as a postcard, and as neat, with solid houses in perfectly tended lawns bordered by the sturdy wooden irrigation ditches, necessary in that arid climate, that kept them green. But what was equally striking was that there were no visible extremes of wealth or poverty, no mansions, no hovels, that at least in appearance a balance had been struck somehow between the demands of a commercial system and the values of a just society. And indeed we learned, in the days that followed, that it was a tenet of the Mormons, whose town it overwhelmingly was, to care for their own, for themselves, with such amenities, held in common, as the irrigation system, town meeting and entertainment halls and a community storehouse, to which all contributed and from which the unlucky among them could withdraw as they needed, all in the interest of a decent society of equals. It was a small utopia, an especially American form of communism, understated and almost undefined; and, though it could not have been as simple as it seemed to a nineteen-year-old buck private from North Carolina, it was inspiring.

After Texas, moreover, the people of Brigham seemed the very soul of hospitality. The tone was set at once. On the night of our arrival many of us wandered downtown to discover the community's annual peach festival in full progress. There were bands and booths, banners overhead and on every lamppost and storefront; streets had been blocked off to permit dancing; we were taken up at once by the townspeople, whose daughters led us into the square. We were a long way from Abilene. The Mormons were abstemious but not—at least toward us—especially puritanical about it. Package stores sold what little liquor was available, usually and often exclusively Southern Comfort, and parties were frequent, though the Mormon girls did not drink at them. This festive spirit lasted throughout the six weeks we spent there, disputing the numerous tales we'd been told of Mormon dourness. For us it was a bit like the great ball in Brussels the night before Waterloo.

But we were at Bushnell for a serious purpose, and most of us took it seriously: the success with which the hospital would function overseas would turn in part on how well we learned to work as a unit. Bushnell itself was a rambling collection of low brick buildings connected by ramps; it specialized in amputation cases, some extreme, many multiple, all serious. Stump and other infections were common and frequently recurrent, and Ira and I found ourselves in a position of crucial therapeutic importance: curing infections almost always depended on the correct identification of the offending organisms; we had to be right. In this we were lucky. The resident technicians in bacteriology were two women in their mid- to late thirties, civilian employees and the wives of officers already overseas, and they were both seasoned and committed; to their mastery of every technique then available for the culture and identification of pathogenic bacteria they added a dedication deepened by their recognition that the suffering which their work aimed to alleviate was the same suffering their own husbands might yet have to face. We probably learned more from them in a month and a half then we'd absorbed in four months of lab school.

Often it was detective work. Our most exciting case—exciting for us, though it could hardly have been for the patient, a double-amputee wounded in New Guinea—necessitated our proving a disputed identification. The patient had developed a stump infection that puzzled the doctors. A swab came down and, following standard procedure, we began a culture on blood agar. The resulting colonies looked familiar; we supposed they would prove to be staphylococci, the commonest of all wound infections. But the microscope said otherwise. There, in the glowing colors of Gram's stain, were the bacilli of diphtheria. I had never seen them except on sample slides and in textbook illustrations, but I believed what I saw. Ira came over, took a look and agreed. So did our Bushnell counterparts. Fresh colonies were sampled, fresh slides stained. It couldn't be diphtheria but was.

The doctors went berserk. Diphtheria grew in throats, not in stumps, they roared; what the hell was wrong with the lab? One of them, furious at our incompetence, came over to say so, and finding Ira and me threw up his hands, muttered his disgust that "a pair of shit-faced adolescents" had been allowed to "contaminate the culture" and stomped off, demanding we do the whole thing over. His fury was righteous; he was a captain and a graduate, I remember, of Harvard.

This was a crisis. New swabs came down and we repeated the procedure. But Ira had been calculating. When the new colonies appeared in the petri dish we not only examined the smears—again finding diphtheria—but transferred two colonies to new slants of media in which only diphtheria would grow. It was not a recipe routinely made and stocked and we'd stayed up half the night cooking it from instructions in a manual.

The slants incubated. New colonies appeared. Each of us sampled a separate tube, made separate slides, took a separate microscope. In a moment Ira looked up, turned to me and with a smile of sublime satisfaction said, "Shit-faced adolescents, huh?" Captain Harvard was called, appeared, looked for himself. "Yes, well," he harrumphed, "the stump *has* begun to sprout a membrane," and stalked off, perhaps back to Boston. A membrane, though usually found in the throat, is a characteristic lesion of diphtheria; subsequent reading revealed—what Captain Harvard obviously did not know—that diphtheria sometimes develops in traumatic flesh wounds.

Not everything we did was that dramatic, but the entire range of our work was interesting and most of it would prove to be useful. On the wards we collected swabs from throats, stumps and a staggering variety of boils, pustules, cysts and fistulas, in the process learning more about the male anatomy than we wanted to know. We took urethral drips and scraped syphilitic chancres. We drew blood for cultures and collected urine in sterile jars. Once we had the grim experience of being sent to the prison ward to take a skin sample from a Japanese POW whose side bore an open wound, four or five inches long, that seeped an ugly green emission, resisted sulfa and penicillin and refused mysteriously to heal. He was resentful, suspicious and sullen, and—echoing the anti-Japanese propaganda with which GI's were constantly bombarded—I was no kinder to him. But his eyes were terrified; for all he knew he was dying in the utmost dishonor; and nowadays I recall with shame my callous indifference to his fear and loneliness.

Presently the 172nd's officers began to arrive. Senior to them all was Colonel Furman Tyner, our commanding officer, short, fat, middle-aged, a peacetime surgeon who now, perhaps to his surprise, was in charge of a staff of more than three hundred—though in fact the complement was never completed until it reached

Shanghai in 1945, long after I'd been transferred elsewhere. He was cheerful and remote, like most colonels, but he made no pretense of being a military man and wandered around in sloppy uniform combinations that would have landed an enlisted man in deep trouble with the first sergeant. Tyner, to his credit, was indifferent to the niceties of army ways, returned salutes with an absentminded wave of the hand and concentrated properly on the complexities of putting a new general hospital in business. He let others play soldier and must have been amused at how silly most of them looked when they tried.

The incoming officer of most interest to Ira and me appeared about the same time: Lieutenant Colonel Juan D. Christopher, a bacteriologist commissioned in the Sanitary Corps who'd be our immediate supervisor. He too seemed elderly, with his sparse gray hair, perpetual pipe and shuffling gait that gave away his academic origin, though he probably was near fifty, and he exhibited an intellectual vigor that was reassuring to newly trained technicians still of tentative confidence, diphtheria notwithstanding. He was jovial, even fatherly, and regarded most army discipline as fussy. But then of course he was not an enlisted man and did not have to make formations or stand inspections.

The sense that we were beginning to fuse as a unit was evident everywhere; and, as the conviction grew that we had a purpose in the war, so did spirit and morale. Griping decreased. Jokes abounded. Nearly every day brought some surprise. We were issued new gas masks in a new model, this one smaller, contained in a smaller shoulder bag and at least more comfortable; we went to the gas tent to be checked out in its use and emerged with the usual watery eyes. Our traditional barracks bags were taken away and duffel bags, stronger and easier to heft, passed out. Our uniforms were checked for wear and old parts replaced. We got new fatigues, field jackets and ominous mosquito nets to be worn under caps or helmets—though a widespread rumor said we were destined for Alaska. Everything was stiff, still unfaded, smelled of creosote.

Promotions were posted. I made PFC and wired home for money to celebrate. No sooner had I sewn on my lonely little stripe than I made corporal and wired home again. One weekend a crowd of us hitchhiked the fifty miles south to Salt Lake City, sought a room at the palatial Hotel Utah and were given a salesmen's display room off the mezzanine where we camped out on rollaways. We partied with the girls from Bushnell and afterward, drunk for the first time in my life, I wandered out onto the mezzanine, euphorically listened to the piano playing Gershwin and Kern across the way and decided, life being so bittersweet with the prospect of an early death, to crash a wedding reception underway in the ballroom. I was blouseless and in sock feet and having a splendid time doing the two-step and fox trot with all the bridesmaids when Ira, still properly dressed and boasting a clearer head, entered and tactfully, explaining with immense charm that there was a war on and we were about to get into it, led me away. The Mormons were relieved but, as usual, forgiving.

Much of our final week or two at Bushnell went like that. At the lab we seemed to work better and better. Preparations for our departure were obvious but smooth. We had mug shots and fingerprints taken and were issued plastic Red Cross cards thoughtfully advising the enemy that as medics we were protected by the Geneva Convention—the joke quickly went round that we could use them to fend off Jap bullets. The whole hospital, though still short of its nurses, assembled for a panoramic unit photograph. It was inevitable that someone would run around behind the slowly moving camera to show himself at either end; the honors fell to Jimmy Delery, a friend from Louisiana who worked as a surgical technician and scrubbed in the OR.

Life suddenly seeming short, many of us fell in love. Every movie wallowed in the sentiment of wartime romance—Robert Ryan and Ginger Rogers, Robert Walker and Jennifer Jones, Errol Flynn and everyone—and now that we had reached the penultimate moment before taking ship we were not to be denied our own. Miles Conrad, though married, moped and held hands with a beautiful blonde, also married, from X-ray. Dick Towey slobbered, in an unsuccessful attempt at drunken heroics, over a girl from pharmacy. At nineteen I fell in love as easily as I breathed, and almost as often, sometimes for as long as a week; and before I knew it, my mind on Nancy but my hormones in Utah, I found myself having long solemn conversations with a Wac sergeant, at least a dozen years older, temporarily training in the pathology lab. One evening we spent hours busily kissing on the hall stairs of the nurses' barracks, where she was housed, but innocence prevailed—I did not quite know what to do next and we had nowhere to go anyway. When she went back to Provo I pined for an hour or two, then fell deeply in love with the girl from the dental clinic who was cleaning my teeth. She was closer to my age and engaged to a bombardier in the South Pacific, and my last few evenings there we listened to records and held hands while she told me how wonderful he was. I thought she was wonderful herself, but when I went to write her a last letter from California a few days later I found I'd failed even to learn her last name.

Casual sentiments, even when intense, were normal in a world at war and in perpetual flux. Soldiers made friends and fell in love with great feeling and often without the cynicism usually attributed to them, only to discover next day or next week that the friend had moved on, the girl was gone. Initial pangs soon gave way to shrugs and vague resolutions to "look so-and-so up" after the war; then, slowly, that gave way to reality and the ships moved on through the night.

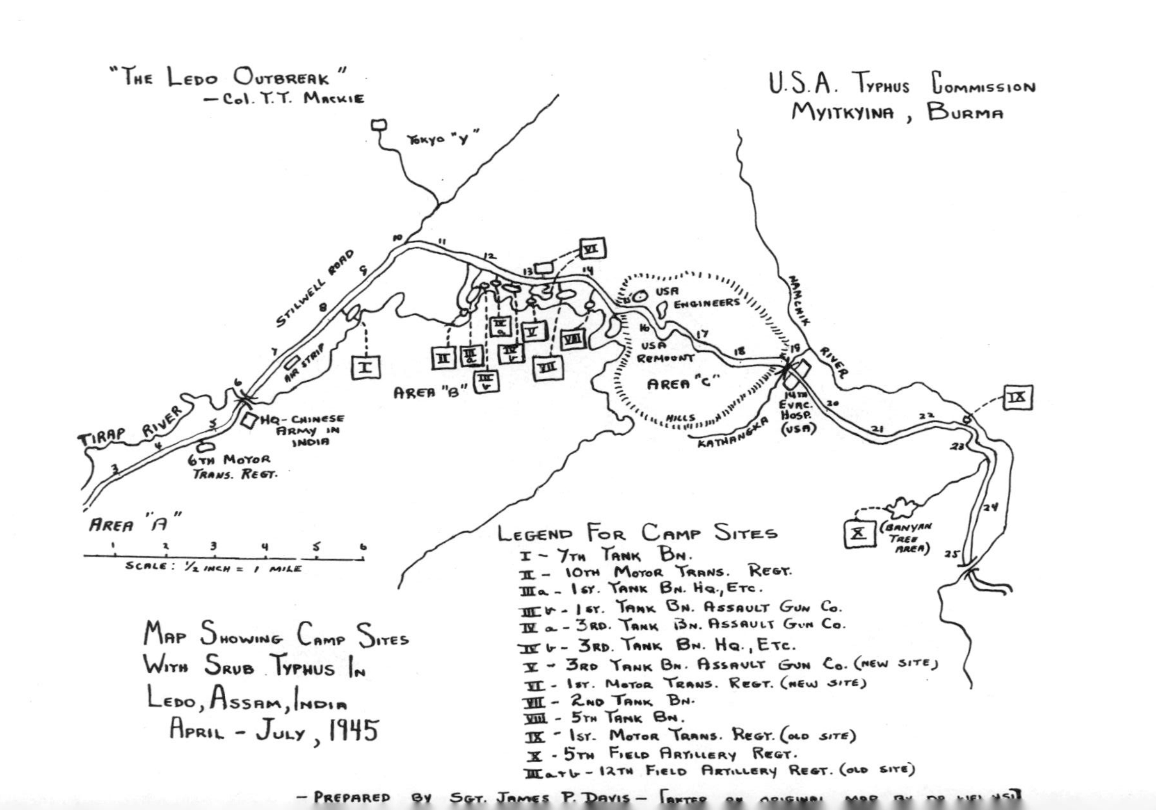
"The Ledo Outbreak"
—Col. T.T. Mackie
U.S.A. Typhus Commission
Myitkyina, Burma
Tokyo "Y"
Stilwell Road
Tirap River
Air Strip
HQ-Chinese Army in India
6th Motor Trans. Regt.
Area "A"
Area "B"
Area "C"
USA Engineers
USA Remount
Hills
Kathangka
14th Evac. Hosp. (USA)
Namchik River
(Banyan Tree Area)
Scale: 1/2 inch = 1 mile
Map Showing Camp Sites With Srub Typhus In Ledo, Assam, India April - July, 1945
Legend For Camp Sites
I - 7th Tank Bn.
II - 10th Motor Trans. Regt.
IIIa - 1st. Tank Bn. Hq., Etc.
IIIb - 1st. Tank Bn. Assault Gun Co.
IVa - 3rd. Tank Bn. Assault Gun Co.
IVb - 3rd. Tank Bn. Hq., Etc.
V - 3rd Tank Bn. Assault Gun Co. (new site)
VI - 1st. Motor Trans. Regt. (new site)
VII - 2nd Tank Bn.
VIII - 5th Tank Bn.
IX - 1st. Motor Trans. Regt. (old site)
X - 5th Field Artillery Regt.
IIIa+b - 12th Field Artillery Regt. (old site)
— Prepared by Sgt. James P. Davis —

With Nancy Smitherman before going to a Christmas dance, 1942.
I am in my V.M.I. dress uniform, which was
comme il faut for dancing.

Laboratory Section, Technicians' School,
William Beaumont General Hospital, El Paso, Texas, May 1944.

With Ira Singer while we were at
Bushnell General Hospital, Brigham, Utah.

The U.S.A. Typhus Commission just before Gene Hughes and I joined it. Colonel T. T. Mackie is the tall man, center rear. Major Gordon Davis is to his right, Captain Bob Austrian third on his left. Caroline Clegg is fifth from the left, Frogg Kailey fifth from the right, among the enlisted men in the front row. Myitkyina, Burma, early 1945.

Major Gordon Davis after ticks.

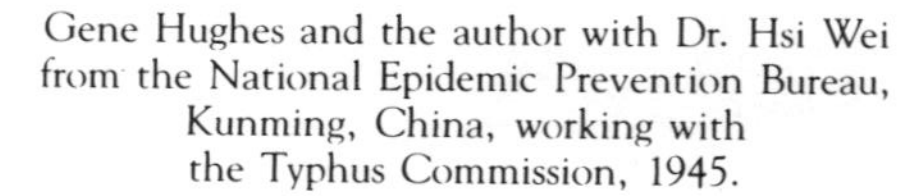

Gene Hughes and the author with Dr. Hsi Wei from the National Epidemic Prevention Bureau, Kunming, China, working with the Typhus Commission, 1945.

Occupants of "Monsoon Mansion,"
Typhus Commission.
Clegg, the author and Kailey.

Badminton.
Clegg and the author.

With Kailey sailing phonograph records into the Irrawaddy.

Austrian, Major Gordon Davis, the author and Hughes
with leopard killed in Typhus commission area.
Myitkyina, June 1945.

971st QM Supply Detachment.
Disinterring remains of American dead at Shingbwiyang, Burma,
December 1945.

The author, Robertson, Zaleski and Hallisey bearing
remains down the slope, Shingbwiyang.

Day of discharge,
Fort Bragg, North Carolina,
April 24, 1946.
My mother and Jimmy McCown, from Lexington, Virginia.

xiii

Camp Anza lay forty or fifty miles slightly southeast of Los Angeles in the flat, arid and inhospitable sands of the California desert. Mountains were hazily visible on the far horizon, but from even the modest distance of a few miles the camp itself offered no more marked a profile than a low cluster of single-level boxes—its barracks, mess hall and headquarters buildings—and a single, dark vertical protuberance, a frame scaling wall outlined like a monolith against the colorless sky; we were to get to know it well. In its isolation and featurelessness Anza could have served as the set for a spaghetti western, had anything so bizarre existed in those days; or it might have been one of those legendary ghost towns of which everyone had read or heard, an abandoned settlement of collapsing shacks that had once been stores and saloons.

Instead of being the last artifact of a dying order, however, Anza was the busy embodiment of a new. Like Los Alamos it was the incarnation of a destructive new society, impersonal, "scientific" and deadly, struggling even at that moment to be born all over the world—not only east of Los Angeles or at Los Alamos but at Oak Ridge and Auschwitz and in the numberless gulags of Stalin's Russia. It was—a term the world eventually would learn to hear with horror—a "processing center." In itself nothing, it created nothing; it prepared its subjects for something else somewhere else.

Nominally, on the other hand, Camp Anza's "processing" was not for death but only for transit, and though that transit might well end in death, as we were constantly reminded, that was no concern of those arranging the "processing." The army did few things efficiently or with dispatch during World War II, but preparing soldiers for duty abroad was one of them. It had a system as firm and as predictable as Henry Ford's, taking men in at one end and a week later sending them out at the other, ready, presumably, for the troopship and whatever fate it delivered them to. In that more insular America only a privileged handful of the twelve million men in the army had ever left the shores of the United States, or even their native communities, and few had the faintest notion what to expect or how to behave, let alone what exotic dangers they might face, when they left the protection and safety of the familiar. Camp Anza was there to make them ready, if ready they could be made; Camp Anza did and could do nothing else.

It did so with a metronomic exactness and in strict sequence. The day of our arrival from Utah our shots were renewed, and to our basic vaccinations for smallpox, tetanus, typhoid fever and diphtheria were now added shots, of controversial value and danger, for yellow fever and cholera, the immediate result being that most of us were sluggish and feverish next day. But Anza had foreseen that and, using the time that would otherwise have been lost, scheduled for it the production of new dog tags and a long, boring lecture, followed by a long, boring training film (through which we snored), on the subtleties and complexities of mail censorship, a subject in which few were deeply—or even superficially—interested. Next morning after breakfast, our fevers past, we were hustled into fatigues, full field packs and helmets and marched to the scaling wall. There we had to swing by rope across a murky pond, climb the wall by further rope, cross the top and come down the other side by landing net, by far the easiest part of the exercise. Still in reasonable shape, thanks to youth and years of sports, I managed the drill without mishap, but many others, older, stiffer and heavier, were less lucky: at thirty-three, in poor condition for such shenanigans, Miles Conrad fell into the pond from nearly halfway up the wall, and Dick Towey never reached it at all, emerging from the water loudly cursing the madmen who devised such tortures. Camp

Anza's non-coms coolly assured both—assured us all—we'd get another chance next day.

The rest of the week passed in similar vein. We saw more training films—on jungle warfare, on camouflage, on venereal disease, on the shortcomings and evils of the Japanese soldier, with stress on his notorious physical and psychological resemblance to the common monkey—and snored again. We were called in one by one and shown our first censored letters home, now scissored to remove all statements, hints or guesses about where we were, what we were doing or where we thought we were going, the big money—mosquito nets and films on jungle warfare notwithstanding—still favoring Alaska; mine looked like the scraps of a paper-doll book and I took them back with a red face. Once again our uniforms and equipment were checked for wear and tear. Once again, this time by booklet, we were shown how inadequate "the Jap" and his leaders and weapons were. Once again we scaled the wall, and once again Dick Towey hit the drink.

During our final three days we were allowed an evening and a night of limited leisure. The first was a few hours in the nearby town of Riverside, where we gawked at the legendary Mission Inn, wandered the streets with no clear idea what to do and settled ourselves finally, as soldiers will, at a bar, only to have the bartender, between prohibitively overpriced drinks, tell us, with the authority only a wartime bartender could exert, that everybody knew we were headed for India.

Since all of us had been threatened with durance vile if we violated security, and had never been told our destination anyway, this was puzzling news; in the end we rejected it as preposterous.

Our last night but one at Anza we were issued overnight passes—again accompanied by solemn warnings about slips and lips and sinking ships—and within a few minutes were on buses into Los Angeles, said to abound in the delights of the flesh. But I was a child of the movies, weaned on them, shaped by them; the movies meant "Hollywood"; and with Larry Elegant from the 172nd, a friend similarly besotted, I set out for its fabled hills. This proved disappointing. The "Hollywood" we'd imagined scarcely existed. Near Hollywood and Vine we glimpsed Schwab's drugstore, closed; Grauman's Chinese Theater, closed; and an infinity of storefronts bizarrely done up as giant doughnuts, hamburgers, hats and coffee cups, all closed too. No studios were in sight, no stars, no starlets. The glamour and the glory, it appeared, were either an illusion or someplace else.

We were rescued by a kindly old patrolman who, recognizing in our downcast faces a distress he'd seen before, pointed the way to the Hollywood Canteen a few blocks farther on. This was more promising, and the promise was kept when a few minutes later I was served a huge ham sandwich by Bette Davis, who seemed undaunted, perhaps even pleased, to learn that I was a Davis too, handed a cup of coffee by Barbara Stanwyck, before whom I was blessedly struck dumb, and shown to a table near the stage by Joan Leslie, with whom I fell instantly in love. Soon the show began. We were serenaded by a beautiful girl named Elizabeth O'Brien, a beautiful child named Jane Powell and a nasal hoofer named George Murphy, all of them the warm-up for the main event of the evening's entertainment: Jimmy Durante and his pianist pal Eddie Jackson in a nightclub act combining music, jokes, extraordinary noise and a kind of manic destructiveness that makes it, nearly half a century afterward, the best "live" program I ever saw. No doubt the presence nearby of the Misses Davis, Stanwyck and Leslie helped.

Our last morning came. After a hasty breakfast in the dark we shouldered duffel bags and whatever gear we couldn't wear and boarded a long train waiting on the Camp Anza siding. By early forenoon we were crossing the Los Angeles slums; by noon we were standing in line inside a huge warehouse alongside the docks of San Pedro's Terminal Island. We could see little but light and movement beyond the open warehouse bays, but somewhere up ahead a band led by an especially aggressive trumpet was belting out the great "swing" tunes of the thirties. Red Cross ladies in prim gray uniforms moved amongst us offering coffee and doughnuts. None of us looked each other in the eye, no doubt fearing panic. This really was it, only now fully absorbed: goodbye to America.

After what seemed forever the line began to move slowly: bags up, bags down. Then it suddenly accelerated, and as we neared the light the music grew louder still and an instant afterward, as his army band swung into "And the Angels Sing," I recognized Ziggy Elman, Benny Goodman's legendary trumpeter, now a sergeant fronting his own group, swinging his own most famous number. It was only a glimpse, however: at that moment I stepped into the sunshine and immediately found I was *descending* a gangplank into the bowels of a ship. That too was a puzzle—in the movies gangplanks always led picturesquely *up*; but I had no time to fret it. "Move your ass, soldier," someone barked, and I moved my ass.

Once into the darkness I simply followed the line, twisting and turning down one narrow ladder after another till we'd reached the foot of the last and the hull of the ship. It was close, crowded, lightless but for a few naked bulbs overhead, its parallel aisles lined with double rows of steel-frame four-decker canvas bunks into which a corporal in neatly pressed khakis fed us, one by one, like sheep to the slaughter. Chance sent me to the top, and as I climbed the frame a foot from the next line of bunks crushed my wristwatch even as a hand from the opposite direction slapped off my glasses, which splintered on the steel deck below. For the rest of the war I squinted to see and never knew what time it was.

The S.S. *John Pope* was neither a navy nor a merchant marine but an army ship—still another puzzle I have never quite solved—and it was large enough to carry a shipment of six thousand soldiers halfway around the world with only one stop for refueling. That capacity, plus the bulk and ungainliness even landlubbers like us could recognize at a glance, gave it the look of a hulking mastodon that would lumber the seas so slowly we'd be forever getting wherever we were going; and our apprehensions were deepened by assurances, delivered over the squawk box once we were at sea, that the *Pope* was so fast we would travel without escort, relying on maneuver rather than convoy to evade the wily Jap wolf pack. It was unsettling to be on a ship operated by the army. It was alarming to be at the mercy of a ship so obviously cumbersome a goldfish could keep up with it. It was terrifying to realize that our only protection was some OCS shavetail's ability to navigate the intricacies of the zigzag.

It was a typical army *SNAFU*, in short, and it plunged six thousand otherwise competitive and even discordant GI's into an immediate and uniform depression. Our despair was not alleviated by the other features of the *Pope* with which we became familiar. The two meals offered daily were invariably mushy and smelly and had to be eaten standing up in a midship mess hall so small we were hustled in and out in a perpetual chow line. After finishing what passed for breakfast we sprinted topside for a quick breath of air, then descended again to find fresh places at the end of the line, there to spend most of the rest of the day waiting to eat once more before nightfall. The troop compartments were so cramped that movement through them, even to the head at the forward end of ours, was difficult; and mounting seasickness left the deck and head incredibly slimy and smelly. To make all of this worse, if worse it could be, all hatches were closed and locked before sunset, and all troops thus locked in, to prevent the escape of light across the inky Pacific waters. Claustrophobia was epidemic, paranoia endemic; it was no surprise when on our third or fourth night at sea a soldier from the 172nd suddenly raced with a scream up the nearest ladder, pounding his fists against the bolted hatch at the top. Calmer heads directed calmer hands to draw him back and settle him down, but no one could wonder why he'd broken. All of us were ready to.

His was the only outburst, but only because the sheer monotony of the voyage drove out all other emotions. We still did not know where we were going or what sort of duty awaited us there, though our daily course was visibly southwesterly, dispelling any lingering notions about Alaska and fueling bets that we were bound for Fiji or New Caledonia or some freshly invaded tropical island liberated by the indomitable MacArthur. When crossing the equator a token sample were subjected to the elaborate japeries and tortures, the duckings and drenchings, that were part of the ceremony initiating all of us into the ranks of "shellfish" and the Brotherhood of the Deep; and eventually all were issued immense certificates attesting to our authenticity. Many spent the dreary days lining the rails as they searched the waves for the first dreaded glimpse of a Japanese periscope. Jimmy Delery, who'd run behind the camera to put his youthful face at both ends of the official 172nd photograph, tried to teach me bridge from the adjacent bunk; his effort was no more successful than mine to teach him chess from a pocket set my parents had sent me just before we left Bushnell. Many of us had stuffed our duffels with paperbacks, which got a busy round of swapping amongst those for whom reading was a balm—I must have read a dozen Ellery Queens, half a dozen Agatha Christies, and I found particular pleasure, still vivid, in Eric Ambler's *A Coffin for Dimitrios*. Meanwhile a rumor swept the ship that one of the largest pinochle games in army history was in progress on the fantail; eventually I wandered up to see, but could make out next to nothing above the hundreds of heads now circling the inevitable army blanket.

Three weeks out of San Pedro, our course continuing southwesterly, someone sighted land and with a scream proclaimed our arrival at wherever it was. This was premature, but as we neared a coast of spires and skyscrapers the word came over the squawk box: Australia, Melbourne—"But don't get your sweat hot. We're only taking on fuel and food. Nobody goes ashore." We anchored well out from land, drawing oil from a nearby tanker. The spires remained silhouettes, the beer unsampled, the virgins intact. Once again—Riverside bartenders apart—security survived.

By now we were nearly as far down under as it was possible to get, but the voyage, still not done, turned calmer after the turbulence of the Pacific Ocean and the Tasman Sea. Then a day or two out of Melbourne, as we entered the warmer waters of the Indian Ocean, we were told our destination at last: India, even as the bartenders had foreseen: India, Bombay and whatever going to India and landing at Bombay might prove to mean. The news itself meant little. An attempted Japanese invasion of India had failed long since. We knew that, and that India was the "I" of "CBI," the most legendary—and most mysterious—American theater of the war, with its distinctive bright red, white and blue shoulder patch displaying a Chinese and an American star above a vertical row of Yankee stripes and its cantankerous commanding general in the floppy campaign hat of the old prewar army, Joseph W. Stilwell. No one had to be told who Stilwell was: his corrugated face and grumpy honesty were the stuff correspondents fed on; but what serving under him would bring no one dared guess.

The tropical heat now made the *Pope* all but intolerable, and adding to the universal misery was the pervasive smell of mutton. The "food" we'd taken on in Melbourne was mostly mutton, it appeared, and mutton in its many forms—boiled mutton, mutton stew, mutton chops, mutton hash, mutton soup—became the invariable entree of our already inedible menu for the rest of the trip. Seasickness, finally dispelled somewhere in the South Pacific, returned in triumph.

We were thus a sorry lot nearing India—exhausted, sick, scared, testy—but the prospect of reaching the end of the voyage was a buoy to cling to, as was the sense, never quite expressed, that we were on the brink of a great adventure; and finally, on our thirty-second night at sea, word was passed by squawk box that we'd raise Bombay next morning. Few slept, and at dawn we were lining the rail. Gulls circled the blue waters of the Arabian Sea. Our first sight was of Bombay's fishing fleet, dozens of tiny barks topped with crescent sails putting out, against our approach, for deeper schools. Then land suddenly took shape against the sunrise, and buildings, especially a huge white arch, decoratively Western, facing the sea: Bombay's "Gateway to India," unmistakable symbol of the British Raj. And then at last, as smoothly as if it were a bark itself, the ungainly *Pope* slid into dock. Below us a tiny train stood waiting, oversized stack puffing steam. Throngs of Indians, all in white, waved up at us. A little band of black men in scarlet uniform struck up "God Save the King."

xiv

He wasn't my king, nor ours, but there was no doubt he was India's, and emperor too: George VI, his firm, prim Hanoverian face staring down at his beloved subjects, and us, from a dozen portraits and posters adorning the walls of the sheds and warehouses and office blocks alongside the Bombay docks. But if it was a prim face it was a benevolent face as well, patient and tolerant, and even the Indians who hated the Raj the most fiercely respected the goodness and courage he and his family had shown during London's darkest hours a few years before and held him and them, the politics of independence aside, in an affection no leader of their own, Gandhi possibly excepted, could draw from them. The hand of Britain was visible everywhere, even as we came down the gangplank of the detested *Pope* finally to touch solid land again: in the dark little bandsmen garbed in British red while they tootled British tunes; in the uniforms and voices of the British soldiers superintending our arrival on British shores; in the numerous trolleys bearing hundreds of sturdy white British mugs of good British tea—grown in India, of course—that passed down our ranks dispensing the sweet milky elixir that sustained the world's most durable empire; in the huffing and puffing of the red-faced British port officials, all in wrinkled white suits and tan pith topees, striding hither and yon shouting orders to which no one paid the slightest attention. I had seen it all a hundred times in my mind's eye, not to mention in dozens of movies like *The Lives of a Bengal Lancer* and *The Charge of the Light Brigade* and *Gunga Din* and the illustrations of an endless succession of boys' adventure books by Henty and Kipling; and, like a man who sees his dream come alive at last, I fell in love with India on the spot. If the reality of India and my romantic notions of India did not coincide I preferred to learn so later.

Later arrived quickly. The din of voices beyond our loose formation on the dock was loud and confusing; and when, tea downed, land legs beginning to steady, we were led to the siding where the train awaited, it became a babble. At the cars we were fed into compartments six at a time, and as we shoved duffels inside and mounted the steps what seemed a horde of screaming Indians surged forward. I had never seen a "horde," did not know precisely what the word meant, but I was sure this was what a horde was. Its noise, numbers and pressure were frightening. Dark hands and faces came through every window; a couple came in from the roof. "Not to worry there," the British corporal at the door assured us. "They just want a bit of *baksheesh*. Shout *jao* at 'em if they get too bad, or give 'em a little stick"—and he obligingly, it seemed good-naturedly, used his own to poke a couple of mendicants away. "You see, then."

The fear passed but the beggars remained. As soon as we shouted one off another appeared, and it was like that the length of the train. Besides *baksheesh*—the world's most familiar term for a panhandler's tip—they wanted to "sell" us cheap beads, trinkets, tin daggers, scraps of brightly colored silk, battered boxes of "real sandalwood, sahib," rotting oranges, rotting bananas in bunches, trays of small cakes spattered in equal parts with powdered sugar and flies, bottles of questionable lime juice, lemon juice, orange juice, bags of colored powder with which to dust one another, miniature Taj Mahals, miniature Mahatma Gandhis, "ivory" chessmen and elephants, "precious stones from the mysterious caves of maharajahs," bent and battered flintlock muskets, brass pitchers and pots, dirty maps of Bombay's notorious red-light district adorned with tinted photographs of dusky girls performing "delicious acts of forbidden love, sahib," cheroots and cigarettes of "finest Indian tobacco, sahib," their sisters, wives, daughters and nieces, all, needless to say, of "most unquestionable Indian virginity," "silver" Moslem crescents, "golden" models of Hindu temples, postcards depicting the ghats of Bombay, Calcutta and Benares, from the superfluity of all of which one could conclude that everything in India was for sale and none of it worth buying. It was a flashing, sputtering Catherine wheel of begging and commerce, usually both in the same breath, and as soon as we realized its harmlessness and got used to it the spectacle seemed endlessly entertaining.

It was the "real" India, in fact, and proved to be endless indeed, then and for the rest of my time there. So did waiting, and ours began then and there when, after taking our places on the train, we spent hours while the train readied itself for departure. The compartments, the lowest class of Indian railway travel, held six of us apiece, often a dozen journeying Indians. Perhaps eight feet across by a dozen front to back, each offered four slatted wooden benches lengthwise on the floor, the middle two back to back, and another two suspended from the ceiling on either side above the windows. We had no cushions and no bedding but our own sleeping bags and were offered none. The latrine was a smelly closet at the front end of the compartment with a hole in the floor surrounded by a steel plate bearing foot markings for the instruction of the uninitiated. There was no seat and we were offered none.

Nor did the train move. We had boarded by ten, eleven at the latest, and at noon we were still standing motionless under the murderous Indian sun being hustled by beggars. It was a long train, stretching out of sight behind us; but it was, to our American eyes, a dwarf. The compartments, of which there were only two to a car, were tiny; the tracks looked as narrow as those of my boyhood Lionel; the locomotive up front, half a dozen cars ahead, was both miniature and antique, an elaborate Victorian toy with its huge red smokestack and tiny cab. Someone who'd worked for a railroad back home promptly explained: India was a narrow-gauge country, and the narrow gauges didn't even match, built that way by British entrepreneurs too busy making money to ensure that their lines would connect: or maybe, a sinister possibility believed by many rail experts, the India Office in London had determined, in the wake of the Mutiny, to see to it that restless natives couldn't move around the country too quickly.

The noise and confusion continued—and would continue at the same pitch till I left India in 1946—but at last, in late midafternoon, railway workers raced up and down the line urging soldiers back into their compartments, the engine gave a toot and a bellow and after a preliminary shudder or two we began to move forward—so slowly the beggars alongside had no difficulty keeping pace with us. We continued like that past the end of the long platform and through the yards, when hands and faces began again to offer us merchandise from the roof. "Bloody fucking Wogs," a sergeant opposite murmured with the natural, innocent air of a man who'd lived in India all his life. American soldiers acculturate quickly.

Bombay slipped past as dusk fell, a blur of tall buildings and crumbling hovels and more people than any of us could remember seeing at once; but the chaos made it difficult to make out in detail. At the city's dim outskirts we turned sharply north, then shortly afterward moved right, northeastward, the course we would follow the rest of the trip. But where the trip would take us we still didn't know and were unlikely, given the army's affection for unnecessary mystery, soon to be told. Darkness had fallen before chow appeared: C rations, a can of pork and beans, beef stew or chicken-and-vegetable soup, another of such dry foods and necessities as hard biscuits, powdered lemonade, instant coffee and salt, pepper and sugar. We ate from our mess kits. Short of burning the train down we had no way of heating the beans, stew or soup and were given none. Short of emptying our canteens we had no water to make lemonade or coffee and were given none. It proved to be a long night—as the countryside ponderously went by, all of us developed heartburn or worse.

Low-grade chronic gastritis was a familiar army complaint, though, and things improved a little when, early next morning, we stopped at one of the innumerable towns on the line. We were able to replenish our dwindling supply of drinking water with sterilized water provided by the British; even better, an old Depression boy, wise from years of riding the rods, reminded us that there was plenty of hot water in the locomotive's boiler. We trooped forward, filled canteen cups and went back to make coffee. The satisfaction proved brief. Instant coffee was in its larval stage of development, alas; ours was "that good G. Washington Coffee" which the crisp Holmes as always urged the patient Watson to share with him at the end of an early thirties radio show plugging that still-new product; and it was terrible. The lemonade was, if possible, worse: the acidic powder mixed with the aluminum canteen cup to produce an especially unpalatable metallic taste. We had no ice, of course, and none was given. A brisk trade with the Wogs began to take shape.

This was richly unpleasant; but India was not, or not for me. I was a Kipling kid, soaked to my eyeballs throughout a boyhood of unlimited fantasy in the tales and poems of brave Tommies and wily Pathans, barracks life on the Northwest Frontier and battle order at the Khyber Pass, all of which I had virtually memorized from endless reading of a stout volume of Kipling's best entitled *Tales of India* in the old, beloved Windermere series published by Rand McNally for the delight of small American boys of the 1920s and 1930s; and I had the *Jungle Book* as well, thanks to a great-uncle, and above all I had *Kim*, whose pageant of the swirling colors and endless excitements of India, its smells and sounds and sudden dangers, our train seemed to me to be displaying like an immense movie as we chugged methodically northeastward toward the center of the country. Fantasy saved me: I was Kim as a boy, Kim as a soldier, am still Kim today.

By now we had maps with which to plot our progress, the rough map of India in the flyleaf of an army indoctrination pamphlet distributed on our second or third day out of Bombay. I kept mine annotated, conscientiously noting our stops and the stations through which we passed; but in greater detail I wrote a running account of our transit of India in a long letter to my parents as the trip progressed. We were still not allowed to post our mail, and this was the next best thing till we could, an epistolary diary of what was becoming, day by day, the great odyssey of my life. The pamphlet eventually vanished as I moved from one post to the next; my mother dutifully numbered and filed the nearly three hundred letters I wrote home during the war, but they too have disappeared, further casualties of American restlessness. The result is that I can no longer pinpoint my daily stops and starts crossing India, though the impressions the trip left remain: the inescapable smoke rising above the numberless huts and hovels of the flat, baked villages we passed, the villages whose simple, subsistent lives are the essence of India; the plains of hard clay stretching away in every direction; the squatting beggars lining the tracks, their hands outstretched; line upon line of men tugging loads of firewood suspended from their foreheads down their backs; friendly British soldiers—"Limeys" still, not yet "Brits"—showing us where, at the rare stops when we were permitted a few minutes off the train, we could buy mugs of tea on the platform; clumps of jungle in the distance; a couple of infantry lieutenants running behind the train in an effort to keep in shape, one of whom would be dead in a month, the other a double-leg amputee; sudden heavy showers followed almost as suddenly by blazing sunshine and the unbearable humidity of evaporating ground water; marching for exercise down the muddy main street of a village, watched on every side by immense brown eyes; the large city of Allahabad sparkling with light against the darkness.

That same night, near holy Benares, we left the train, marched down a steep defile and, after tea from a wagon, crossed the Ganges on a paddleboat beneath the bright light of a full moon; on the other side we boarded a new train in another gauge and proceeded eastward across what is now Bangladesh. Then we turned north again, leaving that train near Gauhati to cross India's other great river, the Brahmaputra, where we were met by still a third train on still a third gauge. The river itself was swift, turbulent and forbiddingly muddy, and before boarding again we were allowed a few hours in the open air. We moved due east through a barren countryside; neither village nor Kiplingesque mosque and temple was visible; the danger of violating security seemed minimal, if danger there ever had been, and we were assembled to hear at last where we were: Assam. It sounded—and was for most of us, who knew next to nothing of Indian geography—as remote as Mars.

Indian pageantry had passed. The final sprint took us almost due north. On the far horizon, beyond the great plain of the Brahmaputra, we glimpsed the snowy peaks of the Himalayas. Then the ground began to rise, to roll, and we moved without warning between jungle and clearing, between sunbaked Indian clay and lush, uncontrollable greenery. The track wound like a snake, following the contours of the foothills. Sometimes, off in an opening between the trees, we'd spy a large white house: the main bungalow of a tea plantation, for we were in tea country now, its steep hillsides lined like orchards with row after row of shrubs. Villages were fewer, though there was no shortage of beggars at trackside; here and there work crews from the plantations turned to wave.

The air cooled. We huddled in our blankets after dark, and a cold rain began to fall. We ate, smoked, dozed awhile as the last day turned to dusk. Just past midnight, with much creaking and clanking, the train shuddered to a stop. Outside the rain had grown heavy, the darkness intense, the only illumination the headlights of a cluster of trucks up ahead. We gathered ourselves and our gear and filed into the void, guided only by flashlights held by ghosts to warn us against the ditches along the track. Then we turned down a road through the jungle, the last lights of the train vanishing around a sharp bend behind us. Our feet sloshed through unseen pools of standing water. I steadied myself by taking the shoulder of the man ahead. The man to my rear took mine.

Finally, without announcement, we tramped under cover, a sort of open barn with straw walls and straw roof. The ground was bare—but dry. "Bed down," a voice ordered from the darkness, and a flickering beam picked out the dimensions of the hut. "Welcome to Ledo, the asshole of the universe." The light went out. We were forty-five days from California, forty-five days without a bath, and you could have smelled us in Norway.

XV

I was wet, cold, hungry, filthy and flabby from a month and a half of inactivity, like everyone; and I was scared, which I suspected the rest were too, though the conventions of the time forbade our saying so. It is more deeply disturbing than most of us admit to have no better than a vague idea where we are, and that, despite the evening's announcement that we were somewhere called "Ledo," was how we were. We awoke stiff and sore from sleeping on the hard ground of the straw *basha* in which we'd been left and staggered outside to find ourselves all but surrounded by jungle too dense to penetrate more than a few feet. The immediate clearing in which our twenty-odd *bashas* stood was crisscrossed with ditches, most six to eight feet deep; the rain we'd marched through obviously was typical.

First impressions are lasting impressions, or course, and may even prove valuable; but ours of Ledo told us nothing except, perhaps, that our journey had somehow ended in the Congo and that presently Tarzan would swing in through the treetops. The non-coms appeared no wiser and we marched off in bafflement to a cluster of *bashas* down the road that proved to belong to a field hospital; there we had breakfast, our first hot meal since leaving the *Pope*, afterward lining up nearby for our first showers since leaving Camp Anza—icy water dispensed by single spigots topping a row of vertical pipes, but the best bath I've ever had. Back at the *basha* we were greeted by troops of teenaged Indian boys, all of them begging jobs as our personal bearers for the princely salary of ten *annas*—perhaps twenty American cents—a week, for which they would fetch our shaving water, wash our clothes, air our sleeping bags and run our errands. Soon, American aspirations to a better life being insatiable, each of us had his own valet. They also liked our cigarettes, which they bummed freely and frequently, smoking them down to what a later generation would call "roaches"; it seemed cheap enough when it got you called "sahib" all the time.

As flattering as that was, however, it scarcely added to our sense that we were helping end the war; and as days became weeks of inactivity while we awaited employment our morale, so strong on leaving Bushnell General Hospital, began to atrophy. It was like being in a replacement depot again: long days of doing nothing but make-work, and precious little of that. Our *bashas* proving rat-infested, we burned them down and replaced them with British tents—each actually two tents, an inner tent with roll-up walls for which netting could be substituted and a fly covering it, with a cooling air space in between, a combination greatly more comfortable than its American counterpart. We built a large latrine to succeed the slit trench that served us for a week or two. We helped put up a mess tent and near it tents for a dispensary and a chapel. We improvised bamboo racks outside our tents to hold our helmets, which became basins for washing and shaving. We stood guard. We played cards and wrote letters. I started a novel. We piddled. Not even the ingenuity of the senior non-coms could imagine enough tasks to pass the time.

Slowly, on the other hand, the details of our location became clear. Assam province occupies the northeasternmost finger of India, extending along the border with Burma on the east to the Himalayas and Tibet on the north, its strategic proximity to both north Burma and China thus providing the armed forces of Britain and the United States an inescapable opportunity for the recapture of the former and the supply of the latter. Much of northern Assam had become a training and staging area for one task or the other as well as for two tattered and incompetent Chinese divisions, whose soldiers American infantry units sought valiantly but vainly to train at Ramgarh. At Chabua and Dibrugarh the Army Air Force operated large airfields for the regular dispatch of supplies by way of "the Hump"—the immense mountain ranges separating Burma and China—to Kunming and Chiang Kai-shek, and both British and American armies commanded glider operations from nearby Assam bases. Ledo, where we were, was the railhead, the end of the line; it fronted the mountains separating India from Burma, and it was there, supporting the numerous engineer battalions and Indian labor brigades building the long overland truck road to China, that the army had constructed, it seemed almost willy-nilly, a staging area of which we now were part. In itself Ledo was nothing in the middle of nowhere, the hub of a complex of dusty roads and a tenth-rate railway converging on a fly-spattered bazaar in a threadbare village that otherwise hardly existed; but the hub and its location were everything, and because they were Ledo had become the most important place in India, perhaps the most important place in Southeast Asia.

It did not look the part. Indeed it did not even look like an "it" at all, being to all appearances nothing more than a haphazard collection, stretching many miles southeast and southwest of the Ledo bazaar, of tent cities, clusters of *bashas*, fuel dumps and, above all, the motor vehicles of the four nations playing their various roles in the war on Japan: motorcycles, jeeps, staff and command cars, weapons carriers, small trucks, the big trucks called "six-by-sixes," dump trucks, tractors, ditchdiggers and the largest bulldozers then in existence, all bearing a bewildering array of flags, colors, insignia and inscriptions marking them as the instruments and possessions, variously, of the United States, Great Britain, India and China. My favorite was a jeep invariably driven by a huge black sergeant smoking a cigar, cheerfully emblazoned with a monster breathing fire beneath whose fearsome head was painted the title, *My Assam Dragon*. The air above Ledo was always black with diesel smoke and always reeked of exhaust, and every patch of open roadside not occupied by tents or *bashas* was littered with vehicles belonging to one army or the other awaiting either use or repair. It was, had we known it, a preview of the American landscape of coming decades.

Ledo was the focal point of a great American war enterprise called the China-Burma-India Theater of Operations, invariably and immortally known as "the CBI," which suffered the burden of bewildering, often mutually contradictory strategic and tactical obligations. One objective was to take part, with Britain, India and China, in the military reconquest of Burma, occupied by the Japanese since 1942. A second was to build a road across the impossibly mountainous terrain of northern and eastern Burma that would permit the steady supply of the beleaguered government and armies of Chiang Kai-shek in Kunming. A third was to maintain air supply of China till the road was finished. A fourth was to keep the Japanese out of India, and still a fifth was to train Chinese infantry for the assault on Burma. All of them aimed at keeping China in the war, though that intention was never articulated to the rank and file, most of whom promptly developed an innocent but inevitable contempt for the "Chinks" and their lazy indifference to the most fundamental necessities of survival. Keeping China in the war was a political problem too, given the deceitfulness, corruption and unreliability of Chiang and his cohorts, whose villainy was monumentally contrary to the heroic propaganda with which the United States boomed China at the time. CBI commanding General Joseph W. Stilwell had his hands full. The common soldiers slogging the muddy jungle trails were not told such things, however; nor, except at the highest level, were their officers; and perhaps they would not have understood them if they had. But retrospect suggests that much of the waste we saw and the confusion we experienced had their real origin in the political ambiguities, uncertainties and betrayals that occurred out of our sight and beyond our knowledge. The CBI was a quagmire of trouble from which no soldier who served there ever fully escaped.

If the CBI had its hub in Ledo, however, it maintained its headquarters in distant, safer and greatly more comfortable New Delhi, where staff wallahs wore proper uniforms, ate the best food in India and slept protected by air conditioning. At Ledo we were under the authority of Northern Combat Area Command—NCAC—and wore rags, ate the customary slumgullion all armies served their forward troops and slept either on the ground or, if lucky, on canvas cots with mosquito nets to give us at least a measure of security against malaria. No actual combat was visible or audible, to be sure, but plenty of preparation for the fighting down in Burma was evident on every side. Malaria and boredom were our immediate enemies. Malaria was one of the perennial scourges of life throughout Southeast Asia and had been so long before the noisy arrival of American troops. Two hundred years of experience had taught the British how to reduce the risk of decimating outbreaks, and the United States Army took their admonitions to heart: standing water was drained where possible and a variety of pesticides, among them a new compound called DDT, helped control the population of mosquitoes; soldiers slept beneath mosquito nets; and everyone took a daily oral dose of a malaria suppressant, atabrine, usually by having it thrown down his gullet while standing in the breakfast chow line. Atabrine had an impressive record but a sinister reputation among the superstitious, many of whom believed it part of a "communist plot" to render American men impotent; and, as would happen with the fluoridation of water in the 1950s, a few went to elaborate lengths to evade the chemical designed to help them. The result was predictable, the first example in the 172nd being a soldier in the cot next to mine who woke up the tent one night while in the onset of his initial malarial attack. He was a Seventh-Day Adventist who'd boasted how he held his morning pill behind a molar, then spat it out, and he was carted away in the inky darkness to a nearby army hospital, never to be seen by us again. I no longer recall his name, but the fearsome shaking of the tent poles and the image of his gritted teeth as he sustained chill after chill are a permanent memory. The lesson was not lost on the few skeptics left.

My remaining tentmates were an odd lot, and we quickly became fast—if, as almost always in the army, impermanent—friends. Bill Voigt, occupying the cot to my right, was a dentist whose prewar degree and practice had won him a commission in the navy, and he had photographs of himself wearing the insignia of a lieutenant junior grade to prove it; but for mysterious reasons he left the navy and enlisted in the army, which did not commission him but gave him the four stripes of a staff sergeant and made him the senior enlisted man in the dental clinic. He was an educated, cultivated man of thirty or so, and his kindness, soft voice and good manners set him apart from most of the rest of the 172nd. Across the tent were three Depression boys, all now men in their mid- to late thirties. Al Flucker had one glass eye, a hernia and a host of other ailments that put him on "limited service" but had not spared him the draft; he was good-natured except when someone failed to pronounce his name "Flooker," and he had an inexhaustible fund of stories about the hard times of the 1930s—riding the rods, panhandling, hobo camps, soup kitchens, selling pencils. John Myers, who was his best army buddy, had a handsome assortment of disabilities too, but he bore them with stoical humor derived from his conviction that nothing, not even Ledo, was worse than Depression America; he was a tale-spinner himself, partial to lurid yarns about the sexual peccadilloes of such silent-screen stars as "Jack" Gilbert, Marion Davies and "Wally" Beery. The third of the trio was, briefly, an army celebrity. He was Larry Sefchek, a big, blond, shambling man who before Pearl Harbor had been a golf pro at a country club next to Mitchell Field, Long Island, where his principal occupation, it seemed, was to play locker-room cards with wealthy members. There he'd acquired or developed a master's skill at hustling, and it was he who'd dominated the notorious week-long pinochle game on the fantail of the *Pope*, in the end winning a pot of ten thousand dollars. Upon our arrival at Bombay, before letting anyone else leave the ship, the army, fearing he'd be killed for his purse, marched him down the gangplank guarded by four burly MP's and ordered him to convert his cash to a money order he then posted home to his mother. He chuckled at his adventure, but to the rest of us he was a daredevil larger than life.

Another set of friends appeared across a clearing facing our tent. The Royal Warwickshire Rifles were bivouacked there readying themselves for combat in Burma; they played soccer in the open space, and we drifted out to watch. Soon half a dozen of them began coming over evenings to share what they called a "feast" with us, always bringing something to go with what we could scrounge: heavy loaves of delicious black bread, tinned bully beef, marmalade, tea, to which we added canned tomatoes, canned deviled ham, sometimes cookies from the monthly packages our mothers or wives had sent. They were expert, after North Africa, at making a little go a long way, and our evening meals around a fire were a welcome relief from the monotony of Ledo. One of them, a grizzled lance-bombardier named Jock McLean, was a golf pro also, in his case at Troon, in Scotland, sometime site of the British Open; he loved the regimental bagpipes, but someone from the 172nd did not and one fine morning put a bullet through the bag. Nothing daunted, Jock fetched needle and thread and sewed the wound back up; and when the Rifles marched off for Myitkyina a few days later the piper led the column, kilts swirling, pipes shrieking their ungodly wails as loudly as ever.

Friendships helped, but they could not overcome our stagnation. Weeks became a month, then two, and still we received no orders. An idle outfit soon becomes a pool of available manpower, an unofficial replacement depot; and presently our vulnerability began to show in absences from our ranks: Ira, who could not drive, was sent to teach Chinese soldiers how to operate army trucks, then to the lab of the 14th Evacuation Hospital at the nineteen-mile mark of the Ledo Road; a friend in a nearby tent, along with several others, was sent to a trucking company readying a convoy to China; for three dreadful days I, who had never flown, acted as a "kicker" of supplies to infantry units fighting in the jungles of northern Burma. This was an initiation I could gladly have postponed: three or four "kickers," strapped to the interior skeleton of a C-47, stood before the open door and, as the plane banked, "kicked" large bundles of food, ammo and medical supplies to drop zones marked by the dogfaces on the ground. It was frightening enough to stand in the open bay held in only by a few canvas straps and watch the ground turn up suddenly as we banked; it was terrifying to watch Jap mortar shells, fired from hilltops close to the drop zones, rise toward the open cargo bay, only to drop away at the last moment. The fact that few of the parachuted bundles landed anywhere near their targets added to the sense that this was a futile as well as a dangerous exercise.

Officially all of us remained members of the 172nd; officially all of us were on "temporary duty" with other outfits; officially all of us could be recalled if and when the 172nd moved or set up shop. But whether and when were open questions, and in the meantime we were being raided of our enlisted men. Morale fell still lower as friends and familiar faces disappeared. Only a handful of our officers had even reached Ledo. One night our entire complement of nurses—whom we'd still never seen—were killed in an airplane crash at Chabua. Then the final blow fell. A day or two later, on a cold, wet afternoon that made the bones ache, we turned out onto an open space near headquarters to hear a special announcement from Colonel Tyner. We sat on the ground; he stood beneath a banyan tree, fat and bespectacled, about as military as an unmade bed.

"Well, boys," he began, "I don't really know a good way to tell you this. I know you've all been wondering when and where we'd be going into operation. So have

I. This morning I found out." He paused, wiped his glasses; his voice trembled. "We won't be. It's all a mistake. They ordered a general hospital like us a year ago, but when one didn't come they made one up out of spare parts from smaller hospitals. Now we're redundant. They don't need us. They may even break us up."

XVI

This was somewhat hyperbolic. Actually three general hospitals "like us" were established and operating at full capacity in and around Ledo, and two of them had affiliations with famous American medical institutions; so Colonel Tyner's remark about the army having created a general hospital out of "spare parts" must have been a lame attempt at a joke to soften his bad news. But the rest—the claim that a requested hospital had somehow been forgotten when the need was greatest—was perfectly consistent with the army all of us knew, and thus probably true. It was *SNAFU* again, perhaps *TARFU* ("Things Are Really Fucked Up") or even *FUBAR* ("Fucked Up Beyond All Recognition"), and it was familiar as lost records, mistaken assignments, trucks that broke down too soon and rifles that jammed at crucial moments. But the fact that none of us was especially surprised did not mean that we were especially pleased.

The prospect that the 172nd had no place to go and nothing to do meant at best an indefinite stagnation, at worst—thus the likeliest future we faced—wholesale cannibalism: we could all wind up driving trucks, kicking supplies out of cargo planes or delivering British tents to new arrivals reaching exotic Ledo in a cloud of *SNAFU*. Before First Sergeant Bill Terry dismissed us, however, I had determined to do otherwise.

The several field and evacuation hospitals and the three general hospitals in the Ledo area were my targets, my hunch being that one of them must need a laboratory technician. It was like looking for a job in a market already saturated with unemployed personnel. The army never sent one man when three could be found, and Ledo bulged with GI's who could not have been as busy as they tried to look. So my first sorties were fruitless. None of the smaller hospitals was short. At the 20th General Hospital, the University of Pennsylvania Medical School unit that was the largest medical facility in Assam, I had a contact in Major Charley Norfleet, an older Winston-Salem man, now a urologist, whose parents were friends of mine: he gave me a handsome welcome when I told him who I was but could only shrug when I told him what I wanted—"We're over-strength as is." At the 69th General Hospital down the road I got a similar answer.

This was hardly the routine army procedure by which "you went where they sent you and did what they told you"; but no regulation I could think of prevented it, and anyway I was desperate both to find good work and avoid bad. I hit the jackpot at the 18th General Hospital, a unit formed at the Johns Hopkins Hospital with a nucleus of Hopkins doctors and nurses. It was located in a remote jungle clearing perhaps eight or ten miles from central Ledo, a pleasant collection of tents and *bashas*, most of the latter built on concrete slabs, far enough from Ledo's smoke, dust and perpetual vehicular noise to be calm and quiet as well as airy and cool. The pathologist running its lab, a red-headed major in his early forties whose name I have long since forgotten, showed immediate interest.

"You went to lab school?" he asked. "And have the spec number to show for it?"

I nodded.

"You know all the basic stuff—blood counts, differentials, sed rates, urinalysis?"

"Yes, sir."

"And some bacteriology too."

"Right."

"What about your CO? Isn't he going to be sore as hell losing you?"

"We're already being picked off right and left. I just want to do the work I was trained for."

He smiled. "All right. I'm short here anyway. Give me your name and number and the rest and I'll see what I can do." Two days later I got orders to go to the

18th on "temporary duty" and the same afternoon a jeep came to fetch me.

I found an empty corner cot in a *basha* near the lab, met my new colleagues and settled in. Atop an old wooden crate by the cot its last occupant had left his latest reading—original trade editions of *The Education of Henry Adams* and Adams's *Mont-Saint-Michel and Chartres*. It was a sign: some inspired sort, I think. I sank into Henry Adams as if into a deep down comforter, profoundly aware that something both important and permanent had happened to my life. His perfect English prose satisfied me as no scientific demonstration, however interesting, ever had; his sardonic detachment touched a nerve that has never ceased since to throb; his contempt for the materialism of the modern world coincided perfectly with the hatred building in me for what the world I knew was doing to itself. I carried both books through the rest of the war and have them still. Whoever left me Adams left me also his lifelong debtor.

The 18th General Hospital was a practiced, assured medical operation. Though relatively few of its original staff remained, its doctors, nurses, technicians, orderlies and maintenance men had a deep well of experience working together, and it showed. Even in the jungles of Assam its wards, service buildings, grounds and roads were clean and tidy. Orderly procedures established in the States and in Fiji, where the 18th had operated before coming to India, were the rule throughout, the result being a commanding air of competence.

Like all field labs the 18th's was rudimentary and might have struck some as crude: workbenches and cupboards were built of roughly finished lumber; water from the tap at the sink could be used only for washing; flimsy cotton netting screened the windows. But the microscopes were good, clean and carefully covered while out of use; glassware was spotless, and an abundant supply was stored in the closet; so were the numerous chemicals, stains and antigens necessary for a general range of lab work; plenty of distilled water and alcohol was always on hand, and the refrigerator and autoclave were in good shape and kept that way even in the vile, humid climate of Assam which quickly destroyed almost everything metallic or electrical.

Of equal importance was the obvious skill of the laboratory staff, who knew what they were doing and rarely had to fetch a handbook to explain an infrequent procedure. Reuben Swartz, with whom I was paired to do the bacteriology, was only a couple of years older than I but clearly more experienced—not in technicians' school but on the job; he knew a lot about tropical infections and was a teammate from whom I was to learn much. The rest, though I knew them less well, gave a similar impression of professionalism.

It proved a pleasant few weeks. It was good to be busy again at something I knew how to do, and the 18th was friendly and relaxed, always competent but rarely military. An outdoor movie screen just down the road showed a changing array of new Hollywood pictures, most of them second-bill *B*s, so that one had nightly entertainment if willing to sit on the ground and fight off the mosquitoes. Like most hospitals the 18th kept its mess hall open around the clock; it was routine to drop in after a show for fried eggs and toast before going to bed. Formations were rare. I had Adams and, presently, Mann's *Stories of Three Decades*, a discovery almost as important. The only ominous note—but a significant one—was sounded by a black GI in a nearby ward: his truck had turned over and pinned him in the subsequent fire, leaving him with third-degree burns over more than three-quarters of his body, a grave injury anytime and in that day of primitive burn therapy a hopeless one; despite morphine he moaned when not screaming, and died slowly. His agony was a signal, had we known it—we could sense it, like so many premonitions, but not quite interpret it. Within a few days we had our answer. The major assembled us and delivered the news: soon, a week or two, three at most, we would close down in Ledo and set up in Myitkyina.

It is difficult nearly fifty years later to convey the horror that place-name inspired. The previous year, as a crucial part of the Allied effort to retake Burma, three columns of volunteer American infantry bearing the ambiguous designation of the 5307th Composite Unit (Provisional), but better know by the journalistic soubriquet "Merrill's Marauders," had culminated a secret and incredibly arduous jungle march by attacking the central Japanese stronghold in northern Burma, the railhead town of Myitkyina on the west bank of

Burma's only real national thoroughfare, the Irrawaddy River. Myitkyina commanded not only the river but a narrow-gauge railway to Mogaung and, across the rolling highland plain, connection with the old Burma Road; and as a point from which to defend their control of Burma it was vital to the Japanese. But the Marauder assault was both a surprise and a success. Then things went wrong. The Marauders, at their peak hardly a regiment strong, had depended on the consolidating support of two Chinese divisions. Amongst the Chinese, however, chaos had supplanted plan. They failed. Japanese resistance proved sturdier than intelligence had foreseen—another instance of America's notorious penchant for underestimating the enemy: Jap bunkers and tunnels were everywhere; their artillery was overpowering, their infantry tenacious; and their internal lines allowed them to reinforce their defenses steadily. The Marauders, soon greatly outnumbered, clung to the airstrip. Three months of bloody siege warfare followed, and the town at last fell. But by then the Marauders had been all but destroyed and Myitkyina was in ruins.

That, told with grotesque simplification, was the story every soldier in Ledo knew, and its grisliness had been enhanced by tales brought back by casualties and by men who'd kicked drops or driven trucks into Myitkyina. They described carnage like that of a slaughterhouse against a field as devastated as that of Roncevaux. The dread the merest mention of Myitkyina stirred was like a fist gripping the heart, and I knew no one who did not quickly look the other way when the move there was posted. But we were going whether we liked it or not; orders were orders. Convinced I'd never see home again, I wrote long maudlin letters to my parents and Nancy unburdening my soul of the endless thoughtlessness with which, despite loving them all, I'd treated them again and again.

The trip was almost as frightening as the prospect. Myitkyina lay only two hundred and fifty miles to the south, but the route crossed the most treacherous terrain in the world via the most hazardous "highway" mankind had ever constructed for heavy and continuous use. It was, in fact, as the army rightly claimed it to be, a miracle of road-building. First the Naga Hills, then the immense Patkai Range—themselves foothills of the Himalayas—threw up a solid wall between Assam and Burma, and both were covered, with few clearings, by dense mountain jungle punctuated by roaring streams that were an obstacle at any time and an often impassable obstruction during the rains of the monsoon, which ordinarily lasted from May to September. The ranges and jungles were so impenetrable that they were largely unexplored and unmapped, and to add to the danger they were peopled by the Nagas, a hill tribe of mixed origin notorious until recent times as headhunters. Christian missionaries had tamed the custom and made sturdy Protestants of the Nagas, who sometimes astonished the GI's of Ledo by congregating to sing old Baptist hymns at their simple services; but no soldier felt wholly comfortable to be at their mercy, which was where the Ledo Road put him. Eventually this too proved a groundless fear, as we learned that the Nagas had served the Allies valiantly by rescuing downed flyers and leading them to the safety of India.

Across this formidable territory American engineers and Indian labor battalions, all under the command of a bristling graduate of Virginia Polytechnic Institute, General Lewis A. Pick, had hacked and grubbed a mountain road connecting Ledo with Myitkyina and Bhamo, near the border separating Burma and China, where it joined what could be rebuilt of the prewar Burma Road to Kunming. The effort had been costly and bloody, interrupted by firefights, landslides and grading problems that would have daunted the Romans; it wound and corkscrewed and rose and fell by dizzying turns, and almost every inch of its unpaved surface was so dangerous to drive that the slightest slip at the wheel could be fatal; but at last it had opened, a land route across the roof of the world, and despite its innumerable hazards and frequent closures for repair we were trucked down and up and in and around it to Myitkyina.

Just east of Ledo, where the railway ended at Lakhapani, the Ledo Road began to climb, winding through the jungle past Chinese and American camps, dumps, depots and remount stations to Pangsau Pass, where at the thirty-nine-mile mark it crossed into Burma at an elevation of forty-five hundred feet. From Pangsau it snaked for eight breathtakingly winding miles downward, the blue waters of Forbidden Lakes glimmering in the valley below, then climbed again past Tagap, at forty-six hundred feet, and Shingbwiyang, the Japs' northernmost supply base in Burma, converted after the Marauders' assault into an American depot, beyond it Jambu Bum, site of a fierce infantry battle, and Warazup, where the greatest tank engagement of the campaign had been fought—in the rainy season a complex of swamps so difficult the roadbed had been raised fifteen feet above the plain to guarantee vehicular passage. Though their names suggested places of substance, none had been more than a village, and combat had left them nothing but jungle clearings whose sole feature was the confusion of war.

Myitkyina, once the principal community of northern Burma, lay still farther south, in the flatter land of the Hukawng Valley, and seemed, as we neared it, merely green and pastoral, the reports of its devastation overblown. But then the road raised the tracks of the old Rangoon-Mandalay-Myitkyina Railway and alongside them we saw the rows of railroad cars overturned and stitched by machine-gun fire, the twisted tracks nearer the station and bazaar. Little of whatever Myitkyina had been remained: a single two-story *basha*, before the war part of the resident British magistrate's compound, inexplicably stood at the center of the village, but only rubble and the tents and new *bashas* of Myitkyina's American occupiers surrounded it. The ditches were still littered with the refuse of battle. Now and then, on some side trail, one encountered Japanese corpses rotting in undiscovered trenches, their rifles and mortars rusting beside them; but Graves Registration had found the American dead and buried them properly in a cemetery close to the residence, the tidy greensward of the compound and the neat rows of white crosses, Christian and Jewish, contrasting dramatically with the general ruin and disorder. It seemed incredible that a nation as great and nominally as "civilized" as the United States could have been so inattentive, so careless and in the end so indifferent as to ask—to command—this waste of its young men, its strongest, perhaps its best.

xvii

We were given no time to ponder that paradox. Myitkyina presented another. It is a familiar feature of modern war that horrifying devastation promptly inspires a frenzy of building and rebuilding; and completing the construction of a new 18th General Hospital became our immediate task. At Myitkyina the Irrawaddy River makes a huge westward bend before turning south again, creating a broad, flat peninsula below the official section of town, around the old residency, which faced the river from what had been a pleasantly shaded bank looking across the water to the great teak forest on the other side. The bazaar and a smaller settlement of *bashas* lay within the peninsula, but the rest was empty enough and open enough to accommodate the many structures a general hospital required; so the Corps of Engineers had located it there and Indian labor troops had begun putting it up. But the site was far from ready for operation. The main buildings—wards, surgery, lab, X-ray and headquarters—were framed, if incomplete, but no latrines, no mess hall and no quarters for officers, nurses or enlisted men. We would be busy.

I was no carpenter, then or later, but incompetence never deterred the army from accomplishing its purposes; and in any case many of the 18th's soldiers, ordinarily garbed in hospital whites, proved to know hammer from saw and nail from screw. Their skills were jackleg, no doubt, but the Depression had taught them not only how to improvise but also not to be finicky about how they earned their daily bread. As I was often to see during the war, the sheer physical resourcefulness of the men of America's working class was immense. Their strength and savvy had helped them survive hard times; they could build airstrips, beachheads, bridges across impassable waters and highways across impassable terrain. A hospital was a cakewalk.

The 18th was a big job for jacklegs nonetheless, taxing the resources of everyone but the hardiest. Concrete slabs supported the frames and woven straw matting formed the walls; but in the lab, to take a probably typical example, we had to build workbenches and install sinks as well as make shelves, cabinets and cupboards to hold equipment and chemicals. The inevitable British tents arrived for the enlisted men's compound—the officers had *bashas* on slabs—but the area had to be cleared, company streets taped out and the tents themselves rolled open and raised. A young Medical Corps captain whose name I have happily forgotten, a gastroenterologist with a reputation for brutal proctoscopy of patients suffering from amoebic dysentery, decided to play soldier, no patients being yet on hand, and proved to be a harsh and unreasonable martinet in matters about which, in fact, he knew nothing. No professional officer would have dreamed of abusing soldiers as he did. He showed a special impatience at the manner in which we erected our tents, making several groups redo theirs again and again while he sought perfect corners with plumb bob and tape despite the fact that, having put up tents before, they knew far better than he how to make them stable. He was a nasty taskmaster whose love of unearned power confirmed the conviction of many that the authority of commissioned doctors should be limited to medical matters.

While the hospital was being finished, and before the first patients arrived, we bathed in the Irrawaddy and ate in a large, temporary mess tent. But within a few weeks we were ready to open and began to receive the seriously wounded and sick from fighting to the south, between Lashio and Mandalay. Most of the staff had worked together so long that, apart from confusion finding equipment stored in unfamiliar places, daily operation resumed smoothly. The patients were far more desperately wounded and a great deal more ill than most of those we'd seen in Ledo, however. Grave head, chest and abdominal bullet and shrapnel wounds were common, and though antibiotics had greatly reduced infection, blood loss and replacement were steady; I did more cross-typing in a few days than I'd done anywhere else. Malaria patients were few, thanks to atabrine, but a ferocious tropical infection new to me, something called "scrub typhus," appeared with noticeable frequency. Like malaria it produced dangerous fevers existing antibiotics did not affect; but unlike malaria it covered patients' bodies with a fearsome rash. My curiosity was aroused.

Though new to me and all but new to the United States Army, scrub typhus was hardly a new disease to the world or to the history of the tropics. It—or something described as like it in the days before the development of modern serological diagnosis—had existed in many parts of the Pacific islands and Southeast Asia for centuries, as I learned by boning up the standard textbook, *Bacteriology* by Hans Zinsser and Stanhope Bayne-Jones, and Zinsser's own memorable popular work on the typhuses, *Rats, Lice and History*, both of which I carried in my overladen duffel bag. Scrub typhus, whose official medical name is tsutsugamushi fever, is an infection caused by a microorganism of the rickettsial family. *Rickettsiae* are smaller than bacteria, but like them and unlike viruses they can still be recognized through an optical microscope; like viruses but unlike bacteria, on the other hand, they cannot be cultured on artificial media, requiring constant transfer from one laboratory rodent to the next to keep a given strain alive for study. The other major rickettsial infections—epidemic typhus, murine typhus, Rocky Mountain spotted fever—are first cousins whose causative organisms are indistinguishable microscopically but differ from scrub typhus in the means by which they are transmitted, in the climates and circumstances in which they prosper and in the details of the diseases they produce in their victims. Scrub typhus is a disease of the tropics and of a tropical geography in which tall grasses flourish; and by the time of World War II it was widely believed—though still not convincingly demonstrated—that it reached human infection by way of mites, which according to the reasoning of the time took the *Rickettsiae* from small ground mammals and passed them on by biting the legs of people walking through the grass. Its initial appearance in the islands of the South Pacific following infantry actions there had been succeeded shortly thereafter by serious outbreaks among the troops fighting in Burma. Soon dramatically ill patients were filling the wards of the field, evacuation and general hospitals of Ledo. Now they were beginning to fill the wards of the only general hospital in Myitkyina, ours. Mortality, moreover, was high.

My interest in scrub typhus was conscious and keen but had no practical aim. The unproven question of transmission—at a time when the insect transmission of such other tropical diseases as malaria, yellow fever and plague was established—was an intellectually fascinating mystery, as was encountering a wholly "new" disease after seeing so much illness and trauma of familiar origin. I was busy, however, as we all were, with daily duty. Once open the 18th General Hospital was operating at full capacity, the only hospital in Burma able to serve a full range of medical specialties. That meant, in turn, that a lot was expected of the laboratory—not only routine blood work and urinalysis but cultures of unusual bacteria, some serology and more autopsies than I had attended since leaving Beaumont General Hospital. I remember with particular vividness being sent to the morgue—another straw *basha* on concrete—to prepare a corpse. The dead man proved to be a large black corporal whose bulldozer had overturned, breaking his neck. His head lay at a peculiar angle, and his flesh, coarse as a rhino's, was dusty and hard; when I went through his pockets I found eight rupees and a couple of unwrapped condoms as dry as old apricots. He carried no wallet, no papers, and I could identify him for our postmortem report only by his dog tags.

I was drifting, bored. Then late one afternoon I got word to report to the major at his *basha*. I found him in tears. "The poor man," he kept saying, "the poor man . . . "

"Who, sir?"

"The president. Mr. Roosevelt. He just died."

And indeed a voice came in again announcing the unthinkable event over Armed Forces Radio from Delhi, and after it a doleful recording of Chopin's funeral march. I choked up too.

Perhaps today it is difficult to imagine that the death of a prominent figure, even a president, could seem so poignant and so personal; but like the major I associated FDR with my country, my family, my fate; I, at least, could scarcely remember Hoover, let alone Coolidge, and Roosevelt had for so long so dominated the nation's sense of itself and its place in the world that he seemed to personify American life, so alive it was nearly impossible to believe him dead. I was as touched as the major, and almost as much by his grief as by the news. I waited, then reminded him of his summons.

"Yes," he said. "I thought you might like a chance at this typhus thing."

"Sir?"

"Well, you seem to be more interested in it than anybody else around here—I never heard so many questions. So here's the deal: you want to go work for the Typhus Commission?"

"Never even heard of it."

"Special research unit directly out of Walter Reed. Does nothing but typhus, which here means scrub typhus. One of our regulars, Manny Katz, went with them last fall but wants to come back now we're in Myitkyina. It's bacteriology."

"I think I would."

"You don't have to. It's a lot more dangerous than here, and anyway I'm not trying to get rid of you. But if I let Manny come back I have to replace him. And it's an opportunity—different, not the ordinary thing at all, a challenge, a chance to satisfy all that curiosity of yours. Besides," he said, "I hear they have the best chow in Burma."

I went to be interviewed next morning. My ride out—in a jeep the major borrowed from the 18th's motor pool—was pleasant. Myitkyina, itself small and all but destroyed by war, was Burma's northernmost community of any size and to its north, though a road led from it to a hill station called Sumprabum, the countryside emptied quickly of organized human life. Small clusters of huts and tiny Kachin villages lay here and there, some near the road, others at a distance along trails only their residents knew; and apart from an occasional team of elephants hauling teak logs from the forest the road was barren. Once past the immediate outskirts of Myitkyina the evidence of its devastation quickly thinned, then vanished, for the tenacious jungle had rushed to reestablish itself where artillery and rifle fire had cut away the leafage and in the process had covered much human litter too. Army outfits—truck battalions, signals companies, a squadron of nightfighters at the north airstrip—occupied compounds alongside the road, but at last, perhaps five miles north of town, they too disappeared. The countryside through which I drove was bucolic: rice paddies to either side, a few Kachin huts with wisps of cooking smoke hanging above them, the immense trees of the rain forest forming an arch above the roadway through whose latticework the powerful tropic sun illuminated what the army stubbornly insisted on calling, despite abundant visible proof that it was nothing of the sort, "the Sumprabum highway." The blue of the sky, the clarity of the air and the gently mottled green and brown of the landscape combined to create the illusion—though this was, in fact, treacherous and dangerous country in which a single false turn could quickly lead to catastrophe in one of the world's densest jungles—that this was the handsome valley bottom, tamed and tilled, of Virginia or Vermont. One could be lulled by such pastoral beauty, such natural peace, and I was.

Nine miles or so north of Myitkyina the road made a sharp turn left; but I followed the sign marked "USA Typhus Commission" and swung right up a short stretch of rising ground, then left again through heavy jungle, descending at last into a succession of small clearings filled with British tents above whose ridgepoles I could see the Irrawaddy gleaming not far away. I stopped at the first tent, identified by a sign as "Headquarters, USATyCom," and as I climbed out a bareheaded little man in khaki shirt and shorts came from under the fly. I snapped him my smartest V.M.I. salute and reported.

"Oh, come on in," he said amiably, not even bothering to return the highball. "We don't go in for all that around here." He extended his hand. "I'm Gordon Davis. No doubt we're cousins."

Gordon Davis was bald, potbellied, sunburned and well past fifty, and he wore the brass leaves and caduceus overlaid with an S that identified him as a major in the Sanitary Corps. "I'm a bacteriologist, in case you're wondering," he chirped on in his high, friendly voice. "I'm a Ph.D., not a physician, but most people just call me 'Doctor Davis' anyway. Which I am, come to think of it."

No one could have accused the Typhus Commission of putting on the dog. The headquarters tent held a couple of rusty filing cases, a field desk with folding legs, a couple of camp chairs and, apart from a litter of papers piled messily on the desk and chairs, nothing else. Major Davis waved me to one seat and took the other.

"So you want to do typhus," he said.

"Yes, sir."

"Tell me what you've already done."

I did: my summers working at the medical school, my courses at V.M.I., my training at technicians' school, my work at the 18th.

"Splendid," he said. "The very thing we need. Manny Katz wants to rejoin the 18th and you sound like the ideal person to take his place in the bacteriology lab." His eyes crinkled above his glasses in what I would come to recognize as a characteristic smile. "It *is* a bit dangerous, you understand. The mortality rate among men who've accidentally infected themselves in the British typhus unit down south is a hundred percent. We'll give you vaccine, but it's experimental, no guarantees. Want to reconsider?"

I wondered that too but shook my head.

"Well, we'll try to keep you hale and hearty," he said, and stood. "I'll have your orders put through, and we'll hope to see you for good in a few days." He walked me back to the jeep. "Oh, I ought to tell you. I'm not the headman. The real CO's in Washington but comes back in a week or two. Mackie, his name is. Thomas T. Mackie. *Colonel* Thomas T. Mackie." To my astonishment he winked.

xviii

It was a wink of complicity, a wink that implied we shared some secret understanding; and I was soon to discover that indeed we did. Blind luck again, unforeseen and inexplicable: I was still under twenty and still hardly more than a kid, but, like the character portrayed by actor Robert Walker in the *Private Hargrove* movies, I had stumbled and bumbled my way into something big, in my case into one of American medicine's most elite and most widely coveted research undertakings of World War II. I was a gangly, gawky adolescent so thin half the soldiers I knew called me "Slim," awkward and self-conscious and despite my V.M.I. swagger still innocent in almost every way that mattered. I had not "earned" good luck nor did I "deserve" it, nor would I have known how had it been possible; yet here, by the unfathomable chance of being in the right place at the right time, I was about to experience what appeared to be one of the crucial epidemiological studies of the war and to work intimately under and with scientists who were among the most expert and most respected researchers in rickettsial disease in the world. It made no sense: all I could say for myself was that when the opportunity came I was prepared for it—and, perhaps, able to see what it meant. Once again my restless dissatisfaction with the routine and stagnation of army life had put me on the move, this time to a unit that scoffed at most army formalities and into work that promised intellectual excitement, adventure and possibly danger. Three mornings later a TyCom jeep came for me, and by noon I was settled and at work.

The Typhus Commission's laboratory, mess and housing tents lay raggedly along either side of a jungle trail that followed the line of the riverbank, beyond which the Irrawaddy, half a mile wide as well as swift, cold and deep except at the sandbar immediately below, rushed south against the spectacular backdrop of teak forests on the eastern side and, rising beyond them far away, the raw blue peaks of the Himalayan foothills bordering China. I took Manny Katz's old cot in a four-man tent directly opposite the bacteriology lab, and after dropping my duffel and musette bags walked over to the lab to report. The lab tent stood upon a wooden platform five or six feet above ground but was otherwise as simple and functional as one could imagine, a single room, screened by netting on all four sides, in which, on plain plank benches built against the walls, whatever bacteriology was done that could be done under such primitive circumstances. Major Davis looked up from the microscope and waved me over to look at a slide. "Your first *Rickettsiae*, I expect," he chirped. "A fitting moment to become a member of the Typhus Commission." Within the bright circular field I saw a cluster of pale pink cells against which a little huddle of tiny dark organisms stood out.

"They look like diplococci," I said.

"Perhaps a bit," he said. "But much smaller."

Then he turned and introduced me to the only other person in the lab, an enlisted man in T-shirt and fatigue trousers named Bob Hull. Bob Hull, a red-faced man near my age, nodded over his steel-rimmed army glasses and offered me a perfunctory handshake but made no effort to conceal his displeasure at my presence. An alarm sounded at the back of my mind, but I barely heard it as the door opened and a dark smiling man of thirty strode in, a captain in the Medical Corps. His handshake was as cordial as Hull's was chilly. "I'm Bob Austrian," he said. "It's great to have you in the Suicide Squadron. Come on and let me show you around."

There wasn't much to see. Tents on platforms similar to ours housed laboratories for entomology and mammalogy, while another served as animal house, with rows and ranks of cages for the gerbils used to maintain rickettsial strains found in the field or drawn from typhus patients; the enlisted men's and officers' tents were spread haphazardly along the trail; and a long screened tent held the mess hall. But apart from the sparsely furnished "headquarters" tent in which I'd been interviewed the Typhus Commission boasted no administrative apparatus—no orderly room, no first sergeant, no company clerk—and apart from a six-hole latrine shared by all, and a barrel-and-pipe rig feeding water by gravity to the washing helmets, it boasted no amenities. Bathing was done, Captain Austrian told me, in the river.

The lunch bell sounded as we finished our tour, and it was at lunch that I met most of the rest of the Typhus Commission, at that point no more than eight officers, of whom the senior, Colonel Mackie, was away, and eleven enlisted men, including me. All of us ate the same food in the same place at rough tables built on the spot, though the officers ate at a couple of tables of their own. The mess tent served also as a dayroom in which officers and men played cards and checkers and chess after hours and wrote their letters home; a battered Ping-Pong table procured God knows where stood at one end, and a smaller table piled high with the equally well-used paperbacks of the Armed Forces Editions stood near it; and though it was as damp as everyplace else in that jungle setting, it was a cheerful, relaxing room. When lunch came in from the kitchen it proved the stories true: the cook, a corporal named Klemasakis, served the best food I'd tasted since entering the army, fresh, flavorful, varied and abundant, with a pie or a cake for dessert almost every day. The excellence of the meals in that isolated scene was, in fact, a subject of constant wonder to us all; even allowing for Klemasakis's skill, and even allowing for the likely skill of the Kachin villagers from up the road who helped with the cooking, the food supplies were no better than what every outfit in the army got routinely; and the only conclusion we ever reached was that yes, Klemasakis was a great chef, and yes, his Kachins had a knack for fish and rice and vegetables, but that most important of all, they only had to cook for fewer than twenty men at a time. This was no "regimental" mess, praises be, and it never let us down: good chow to the last meal the Typhus Commission served.

Getting my new companions straight would take longer than liking the food, however, and in an outfit so small and so specialized it would be important. At first I simply shook hands around as I was introduced, not really taking in more than names: Lund, Clegg, Sundermeyer, Kailey, Weber . . . and the officers: Fuller, Stager, Girsham, the latter a swarthy, vaguely Oriental man of middle height, already past forty but rippling with physical power, with a British accent that was still not quite British. While we were eating someone told me, voice lowered, that this was the legendary "Captain Jack" Girsham, famous for his prewar feats as a big-game hunter and keeper of Burma's animal preserves and even more famous for his exploits as trailblazer and point man for one of the columns of Merrill's Marauders, a jungle fighter, captain in the British forces, whose skills in the "bush" were surpassed only by the savagery with which he'd killed Japs. He'd lost his wife and children as they'd fled the advancing invaders of 1942 up the treacherous refugee trails of northern Burma, lost them utterly, even the whereabouts of their bones, so that his ferocious spirit was thus animated by a personal as well as a patriotic purpose. To me, for all his storied valor, he was charming, courteous and almost exquisitely gentle, and it was not long before I realized that he was the most popular figure in the Typhus Commission.

The real working day began next morning and almost immediately assumed a form that lasted as long as the outfit itself lasted. A big breakfast—we could even have fresh eggs if we traded cigarettes for them with Klemasakis's Kachins—sent us off to the various labs. At ours I soon learned the routine of dissecting dead gerbils, examining smears from their livers and kidneys under the microscope, then grinding the organs into a paste that was finally injected into fresh gerbils, a procedure, given the impossibility of culturing rickettsial strains on the artificial media by which bacteria were maintained, that permitted the perpetuation of scrub typhus *Rickettsiae* for study purposes. I grew adept at staining slides and identifying the organisms microscopically; but Bob Hull was jealous about dissection, insisting again and again that he knew the technique better than I could ever hope to, and soon I gave up trying, unwilling to fight but puzzled by his obvious hostility. He did not know me well enough to dislike me.

Major Davis and Captain Austrian were wonderful to work under and be with, on the other hand, always good-humored, kind personally and generous in explaining what we were doing and why. The point, Major Davis said repeatedly, was to "incriminate the mite"—to prove beyond dispute, if possible, that a particular species of mites, perennially suspected of being the vector of scrub typhus, actually did the deed. Thus the officers and men in entomology combed the high grasses for mites, which they classified and saved, while the mammalogy people sought ground animals in the rain forest—along the jungle floor—in whose bodies the offending pathogens lay waiting. Davis hinted with his elfin wink, however, that he still suspected ticks, as in Rocky Mountain spotted fever, and would go on hunting and studying them till the mite advocates proved him wrong.

Afternoons were slower. The tropic sun of Burma is hot most of the year, and as the spring monsoon approaches the midday heat becomes intolerable to work in. After Klemasakis's sumptuous lunch nearly everyone in the Typhus Commission lay down to read or sleep—one day I was awakened by an elephant's trunk at my cheek—and for a couple of hours, until the worst had passed, little was done. Afterward the entomologists sorted their specimens, the grounds crew of Kachins worked at maintenance and repairs and with the routine bacteriology done we did odds and ends. Major Davis liked to go looking for ticks, believing them easier to turn over in midafternoon, and I often went with him to drive, dig and cluck appreciatively at his delighted discoveries. Once, at his bidding, I drove south with him on a five-day trip all the way to Mandalay, still dangerous from the fighting and from Chinese and a few Japanese deserters in the jungle. We stood together at the crest of Mandalay Hill overlooking the devastated city below, a smoky plain of flat rooftops of corrugated iron, all, except for a cluster of pagodas in the distance, that remained after weeks of shelling and gunfire; and he, usually so cheerful and voluble, only shook his head at the waste. On our return trip we spent a night at Namhkam at the mission hospital created by Gordon Seagrave, the famous "Burma surgeon," as he also entitled his best-selling autobiography; he was by then a lieutenant colonel in the Medical Corps and busy rebuilding the place from the ruin the Japanese had left it, and at dinner he regaled us with tales of their depredations and atrocities. I thought him vain and autocratically snappish with his Burmese nurses, whom he'd trained himself; but his little hospital had greatly bettered the health of the hill people around him, and he and his nurses had performed heroically as a front-line surgical unit during the siege of Myitkyina. He'd earned his egotism.

Captain Austrian liked to roam after siesta too, usually to hunt crows along the trails nearby, and he often had me drive him. Burma being British, we had to use the left lane, such as it was, which after a few days I found easier than I'd expected; but I always looked the wrong way at critical moments, and once, jamming to a stop as he aimed his shotgun from the other side of the jeep, I heard a screech of brakes and an instant later saw in the mirror a speeding British lorry, which then made the horror complete by slamming into our rear end just as Austrian's gun fired. No one was hurt, as it turned out—only our jeep, which we returned to the TyCom motor pool badly bent. I spent an uncomfortable hour next day explaining what had happened to the MP's in Myitkyina, and Bob Austrian told me years later he realized then and there that I was deeply, irredeemably absentminded. I preferred to regard myself as admirably concentrated.

A late-afternoon plunge in the brisk Irrawaddy, blending both British and American uses of the word "bathing," generally ended the day. The bluff upon which the Typhus Commission lay ended in a narrow strip of sand at the waterline; but twenty feet out a long sandbar offered a more attractive beach, and unless the water was high, as it became at the peak of the monsoon, it was easy to cross the shallows to it. The water was cold and its currents were rapid and could be dangerous; but it was clean too, here in northern Burma, above the pollutions of towns and cities and the carelessness of human development: not safe to drink, perhaps, but against a scene of violence and destruction it seemed clear and pure, still undefiled by the innumerable horrors mankind had inflicted on the world.

Sometimes we had a movie at night, eventually several a week, sixteen-millimeter prints of new Hollywood pictures; they were projected against a sheet in a clearing above the labs and quarters, and the Kachins from the kitchen and grounds crew and village crept up to watch, squatting in the darkness, as did—or so the Kachins told us—Chinese and Japanese deserters lurking in the nearby bush. Distribution by the recreation office in Myitkyina was so unpredictable we rarely knew what we'd see next, and a lot of it was "B" stuff aimed at filling the lower bill of double features back home, but most of us were so homesick we welcomed even the silliest of them. We got the best movies too, generally months before their scheduled release in the States, *Laura* and *Meet Me in St. Louis*, not to mention a pretentious turkey purporting to show the notorious draft dodger Errol Flynn recapturing Burma single-handedly, which drew the inevitable catcalls; but the picture I remember best was the wonderful Howard Hawks version of Raymond Chandler's *The Big Sleep*, which we saw again and again, night after night, perhaps in the end as many as twenty times. Temporarily cut off from Myitkyina, we had nothing else, and before it was over I could recite Humphrey Bogart's lines—and did—before he delivered them on-screen. After the war I saw it again and knew it so well I was astonished to realize that between Burma and North Carolina Hawks had reshot one important scene substituting another actress for the "starlet" I remembered seeing play the part of Mona Mars in an isolated jungle clearing north of Myitkyina half a world away.

xix

Mackie came back a week or two before V-E Day: Thomas T. Mackie, *Colonel* Thomas T. Mackie, as Major Davis had winkingly identified him, the headman of the Typhus Commission. A delayed entrance often raises expectations by enhancing a figure's legendary quality, as every playwright knows; and as a principal actor in our unfolding drama Mackie had acquired by his protracted absence in Washington a profound air of mystery, even of glamour. The fact that the older hands had said little about him beyond a cryptic aside here and there only thickened it. "A bit of a gamecock," I remember Sundermeyer saying. "He glitters when he walks," Captain Austrian said, borrowing a line from Robinson's "Richard Cory." Kailey said simply, "You'll see."

I was thus prepared for someone larger than life at the very least, and I was not disappointed. Mackie had flown into Myitkyina from Ledo and Martin, the official TyCom driver, had met him at South Strip; but on reaching the compound he'd disappeared into his tent and made no general appearance till supper, when—like a conductor taking the podium and facing his orchestra—he strode alone into the mess tent, gave a cheery wave around and seated himself at one of the officers' tables. But then, one of them obviously having told him a new man was present, he bounded to his feet and dashed over to my table to shake my hand with extraordinary energy.

"Damned fine to have you among us, Pax," he said, already knowing how I was called. "The very thing! Just splendid!"

I was taken aback—colonels, in my experience, were not given to such overflowing demonstrations of friendship with enlisted men, tending instead to formality and correct but detached courtesy—but Mackie would work his charms. By then in his early fifties, he looked every inch the warrior and had done almost everything imaginable to underscore that image. Though most of the rest of us dressed as casually as the law allowed, in T-shirts and baggy khaki or fatigue trousers and muddy GI shoes, he was decked out in immaculately tailored and *pressed* khakis, with a nonregulation British bush jacket for a shirt and above its left upper pocket a row or two of ribbons signifying his decorations not only from our war but from World War I, in which, it appeared, he'd served with considerable valor. The bowl of a pipe protruded from the opposite pocket, and his whitening blond hair was cropped almost as short as a Parris Island drill instructor's. But what was most striking of all was his height: at six-feet-three or -four, and slender to match, he towered above everyone else in the outfit but Kailey, who stood six-six even if he was a buck private. Mackie could not have minded. His height and costume only supported his aristocratic domination of the scene. I thought instantly of Neil Hamilton, the "Arrow Shirt man" of silent movies, with a pinch of Walter Pidgeon thrown in for good measure. The piercing blue eyes, the long supple figure, the commanding voice—Mackie was a colonel straight out of MGM.

Supper done, we gathered at the end of the tent. Mackie stood by the Ping-Pong table. He had important news, he said. First, now that the war in Europe was drawing to a close our work would assume a greater importance in the eyes of the Washington medical bigwigs: we weren't just the Army Typhus Commission, we were the United States of *America* Typhus Commission, and we'd draw from hither and yon, wherever we needed, for more men, more typhus experts, more equipment, a better layout. He named names: Jellison, Kohls, Bell, all experienced scientists from the Rocky Mountain Laboratory of the United States Public Health Service in Montana; Dr. Hsi Wei, a Harvard protégé of Hans Zinsser's, now a leading researcher in rickettsial disease, would be coming over from the

National Epidemic Prevention Bureau in Kunming. A larger enlisted contingent was on order, he said: more technicians, a clerk or two to handle the paperwork, a horse-handler to supervise the making of vaccines. We'd get solid buildings to work and live in, running water for the labs, a proper shower room.

Second, Mackie said with a dramatic elevation of his eyebrows, and far more pressing, immediately, on us all, a major new outbreak of scrub typhus had just been recognized among the Chinese troops occupying the complex of campsites through which I remembered passing fifteen miles out of Ledo. A pathologist at the 14th Evacuation Hospital had done some "splendid" detective work confirming the determination, performing dozens of autopsies in the process. "A priceless opportunity," Mackie told us, his eyes searching ours. "We'll want to send in a team at once. We mustn't let the chance pass to work at such a concentration." Then, relaxing a bit, he smiled and said, "It's going to take all we've got. But I want to make you a solemn promise. I'm going to see to it that you get the promotions you deserve, particularly you enlisted men; you've waited patiently and for a lot longer than was right." He paused a moment, lost, it seemed, in some solemn thought beyond quotidian trivialities; he gave another quick, tight smile. "I mustn't reveal any military secrets, of course"—implying he knew some—"but all of you must realize that soon enough we're going to have to play our parts in the invasion of Japan. It's going to be a big show, bigger than most of us can quite take in, and I know I can count on you. So I want, as I say that, to make you another promise: when it's all over at last, when the Jap's beaten and gone to ground, we're all going home together, as a unit, and claim the credit we've earned."

It was a consummate performance, flamboyant, theatrical and exciting like everything else about Mackie, a bit of St. Crispin's Day in Burma's heart of deepest darkness. I had never heard anything like it outside the adventure movies I had doted on in boyhood; it blended *Beau Geste* and *The Charge of the Light Brigade*, yet was more effective because more immediate. Utterly innocent of manipulation and weary of the usual banalities of army life, I went to bed stirred as I had rarely been; and when next day I was summoned to the headquarters tent I was atremble with expectation.

"Yes, do take a pew, dear boy," Mackie said, packing his pipe from a leather pouch and waving me to the other camp chair. "I wanted to tell you I was in Winston-Salem last week and bring you the warmest salaams and felicitations of Alice Gray, who knew you were here—I believe you call her Polly." Alice Gray was a spinster friend of my parents with whose own parents my father had roomed for a year before marriage; her father and brother were doctors but dead many years, and though she was a member of the larger Gray family that all but ruled Winston-Salem I could not imagine the connection and didn't dare ask. He maintained the mystery. He paused, relighted and let my surprise sink in—it was not as if, after all, Polly Gray were a family intimate, and the coincidence was bizarre. He said, "Yes, she seems quite fond of you and your people," then, in a sudden shift, "I do hope you'll be up to a romp down the road. I want to send you to the 14th Evac to work on the Ledo outbreak; you and Hughes, and perhaps an officer in a few days. Take smears at autopsies. Make slides. Start strains in the gerbils. You think you can handle that?"

By now I was dumbstruck and could do little better than nod, certain that my Adam's apple must be bobbing.

"Good show, then," Mackie said, all broad smile and twinkling eyes. "It's a splendid opportunity, you know, and you're bound to have a jolly time *and* learn lots." He rose, hand extended. "Off you go. Pack your kit. You catch the shuttle first thing tomorrow."

The trip to Ledo was, as always, bumpy and nerve-racking; and to its customary hazards Gene Hughes, my companion, added an element of derring-do that I found nearly as unsettling. The Air Transport Command provided, besides its numerous flights across "the Hump" to China, a daily shuttle between Ledo and Bhamo, with a stop at Myitkyina; it crossed the Naga Hills, themselves perilous at all seasons, and it used battered C-47s, serviceable cargo planes that had won a great reputation for durability but were uncomfortable and seemed more fragile than they were. To expedite loading and unloading under invariably difficult conditions—especially for "kicking" drops to ground troops, which I'd done a few months earlier—the flyboys had ripped off their doors, so that passengers got a sickening view of jungle and mountain as the planes dipped and snaked their way through the passes, often discovering themselves well below the Ledo Road as the plane slithered its switchbacks along the complex contours of the Patkais. That was for Hughes the irresistible dare. For most of the flight he insisted on standing at the open door as casually as if he were on his own front stoop, one hand against the doorframe, the other at his hip; and my whinnied pleas that he come back inside and strap himself to a bucket seat, like a normal person, only drew shrugs. An infantry lieutenant still carrying his carbine was the only other passenger; he chuckled.

Gene Hughes was even newer to the Typhus Commission than I, a tent mate but still hardly known. He was a leathery, sinewy, deeply tanned man of thirty, about my size but physically much tougher, thanks, perhaps, to the outdoor life he'd led in his native Montana, where, in the Bitter Root Valley, he'd grown up and then, as an adult, worked in the Public Health Service laboratory alongside Major Davis and those other expected arrivals, Bell, Jellison and Kohls, whose names he usually uttered as if they were one. He was married, had children, was richly experienced in rickettsial research; but his transfer to the Typhus Commission was as much a lucky fluke as mine: he'd been in a M*A*S*H unit down south of Mandalay when Davis discovered it and requested him. He looked a lot like the younger Walter Brennan and knew more about the bush—flora, animals, insects, the crafts of the woodsman—than anyone I'd ever known. It buoyed my confidence to be with him—except when he stood in the open door of a C-47 flying the shuttle.

The 14th Evacuation Hospital straddled the Ledo Road along a deep draw in the Naga Hills nineteen miles southeast of Ledo bazaar. The ravine was ripe with the growth of the jungle, which threatened at all times to reclaim the clearing in which the hospital lay; maintenance crews struggled daily to restrain its tenacious creepers, which pushed stubbornly toward the feeble light, and no one could doubt that within a few weeks of the hospital's abandonment the site would show few signs of its erstwhile occupation. Apart from dozens of British tents alongside the road and haphazardly up the slope in either direction the hospital looked mostly like a garbage dump, another instance of the army's carelessness and indifference in occupying the property of another country. The dominant impression was of planlessness, randomness. But the impression was misleading: in its daily operation the hospital itself was a model of thoughtfulness and order.

Gene Hughes and I got there by a jeep borrowed from the motor pool at the Ledo airstrip, though to our disappointment we had to surrender it once we reached the 14th. We'd brought a couple of dozen gerbils in a huge flat box divided on one of its big sides into a grid of tiny cages; the difficulty was that when the screened lid came off gerbils erupted in every direction, like popcorn. They were small, fast and so brown they were hard to spot, and they were difficult to catch if they got away from you. They also had sharp front teeth which could sink into a finger before you knew what was happening; we had to wear heavy gloves to handle them. But Gene was as adept at corralling lab animals as he was at everything else, and soon we got them into the conventional cages the 14th had readied for us. Then we went looking for the man who'd discovered the outbreak.

Major Bob Roberts proved to be in his tent and already, in early afternoon, fairly drunk, though perfectly coherent. Wearing only khaki shorts and muddy GI shoes, he was a fair, stocky man in his late thirties, and sitting on his cot he filled us in. He'd begun to find suspicious scablike lesions on the calves and inner thighs of Chinese patients who'd died in the throes of fevers no one could account for in ordinary terms; the gross autopsies had been followed by tissue smears as well as sections. So many had turned up *Rickettsiae*—which he'd never seen except in textbook photos—that he'd asked the 20th General Hospital to do serologies; they'd confirmed his original hunch that he'd found scrub typhus. The rest was simple logic: he'd pinpointed the staging areas of the dead Chinese soldiers and determined all were from a cluster of combat units not only near one another but near fields of tall grass. Roberts smiled, took another sip from his bourbon bottle. "QED," he said. "So here you guys are and here I am going home at last after two fucking years in this asshole jungle."

We were there two weeks, perhaps three. Gene and I did the lab work Mackie had specified, and at some point Clegg, another tent mate, flew down to collect mites. The 14th Evac lab helped. Gene was able to show Major Roberts a few tricks about staining *Rickettsiae* and identifying them under the microscope. We took autopsy samples from scrub-typhus victims and initiated strains in the gerbils; when those gerbils died we transferred the strains to healthy gerbils, who then grew sick and died too. We kept careful notes tabulating cases and strains. Toward the end of our stay, when the outbreak appeared to be abating, Gene and I spent a day among the Chinese troops in whose compounds the fever had arisen, infantry and artillery, and talked at length, when we could, with their officers, though the only thing we learned was that one of the generals, who'd spotted my silver college ring, was a V.M.I. graduate, class of 1927. This provoked a great celebration and more drunkenness than the United States Army would've found seemly; but Chinese generals, I discovered, did what they liked.

Yet in the end it all came to nothing. The rickettsial strains we'd so carefully maintained were flown back to Myitkyina only to be put into fresh gerbils and sent on to Washington, which promptly let them die. Our slides were good but revealed nothing not already known, and eventually they disintegrated. No vaccine resulted. No *Rickettsiae* were found in Clegg's rich trove of riskily collected mites, so the theory of mite-bite transmission remained unconfirmed.

In time I would come to realize that our entire experience in the Ledo outbreak was a microcosm of the Typhus Commission's labors in Burma; immediately, however, a more tragic disappointment occurred. Major Roberts did not get home, not quite. He was an able pathologist, not only intelligent and experienced but intuitive and deeply curious, and that combination of gifts might have made of his hundreds of case histories and autopsies one of the classic bodies of medical data in the field of tropical disease. But that opportunity, like so many raised by World War II, was lost to bureaucratic indifference, personal ambition and the vagaries of wartime. Roberts was like many of the men I came to know who ended broken by Burma, by the CBI itself—burned out, in the phrase of a later day, by being isolated too long, by sinking into a depression caused by heat and rain and the endless woes of everyone they knew, by the grinding hopelessness of jungle warfare. He wound up drinking too much and becoming careless in his work, performing autopsy dissections half-naked and with his hands unprotected by rubber gloves. A few days before his departure for the States he did one more. Evidently fluid from an internal organ spattered his fingers and a small scratch admitted infection. The flight home took weeks, and when at last the plane landed in Miami they took him off, to the horror of his waiting family, in a body bag.

XX

Germany fell while we were still at the 14th Evac, but celebration of V-E Day was muted. The defeat of the Nazis was welcome news, of course, but for soldiers and sailors fighting the Japanese the war continued and grew even uglier as Allied forces neared the enemy mainland. No one serving in the South Pacific or in Southeast Asia any longer believed American propaganda or doubted the skill, tenacity and courage of the Japs, and the prospect that eventually most of us must take part in the inevitable invasion of Japan effectively dampened any high spirits aroused by the end of the war in Europe. If until then the CBI had been a backwater, now emphasis must shift our way.

I turned twenty, flew back to Myitkyina, found the Typhus Commission enlarging and on the point of occupying a new compound. While we were away the engineers had completed our new labs and quarters a few hundred feet up the slope on flatter ground, and within a few days of our return we moved. The new laboratory building was long, low and stood on a slab; framed and screened, with a pitched roof of canvas tarps, it was divided into big square sections that greatly enlarged our working space, and it boasted running water fed by gravity from a reservoir on higher ground; the animal house and a sterilization chamber with an autoclave lay a dozen yards away. Three similar buildings—one for the officers, two for enlisted men—provided quarters but were elevated well above ground to protect us from flooding. A mess hall was across the road, there was a true headquarters building at last and in the center of it all we had a big open shower building drawing on the same gravity feed that served the laboratories. The structures were crude and the water was cold, but we all felt we'd come up in the world. Kailey, a master scrounger who went into Myitkyina for mail and groceries almost daily, even produced a red supply parachute he'd "liberated" from the Air Transport Command at the north strip; we hung it from the ridgepole and its billowing skirts, tacked to the studs at the corners of the room, gave us a bit of color, eventually too much.

The newcomers nearly doubled the size of the Typhus Commission. Among them were additional lab technicians, drivers, a veterinary technician to supervise the animal house, two cooks to help Klemasakis, a first sergeant to run the new orderly room, an administrative second lieutenant to make a nuisance of himself and a suspiciously shaky doctor whose redundant duty was to give shots and hand out atabrine and aspirin—all of which Captain Austrian had done till then without fuss or anything so elaborate for a small outfit like ours as a "dispensary."

Conspicuous among the new faces were those of four, all either officers or accorded officer status, whose names were widely known in tropical medicine. Three were old hands from the same Public Health Service lab in Montana where Major Davis and Gene Hughes had worked. Glen Kohls, now a major in the army, and Bill Jellison, wearing major's insignia but still technically a civilian government employee, were renowned epidemiologists who had hunted lice, fleas, ticks and mites the world over. Kohls was short, wiry, gray and bespectacled, the perfect stereotype of a college professor, but Jellison was big, burly, dark and rumpled and would more likely have been mistaken for a truck driver. John Bell, the third from the Montana lab, was an army captain, a bacteriologist who'd worked epidemics everywhere, lean, gently spoken, a little stooped and deeply preoccupied most of the time; from Gene, who'd worked closely with him back home, I knew he'd managed to contract most of the diseases he'd investigated, though he rarely spoke of such things. The fourth newcomer was in many ways the most interesting of the lot: Dr. Hsi Wei, from the National Epidemic Prevention Bureau in Kunming, a Harvard medical graduate who'd apprenticed the great Zinsser before returning to his native China; he was of medium build and spoke an English so lightly accented a blind man would hardly have guessed his nationality. He was both extravagantly courteous and markedly friendly and often entertained us with tales of medical practice in his—as it seemed to us—exotic land, though none of us, true believers in the scientific medicine of Britain and America, could quite accept it that acupuncture worked, could even be employed for anesthesia.

If our ranks were growing, however, cliques were tightening. Those of us who'd occupied the tent camp down the slope—even Gene Hughes and I, the last men to come over before the move—became, at least in our own eyes, the "old" Typhus Commission, the true devotees of its holy mission and Spartan simplicities; and in this self-anointed priesthood we were joined by the Hull-Lund-Weber-Sundermeyer clique, who until then had seemed to regard us, with unconcealed hostility, as rowdy adolescent intruders in their private world of scientific purity. Among the officers such divisions were less visible, and the undeniable prestige of Bell, Jellison and Kohls insulated them against many of the resentments and jealousies we enlisted men exhibited so plainly, while Dr. Hsi was in a class by himself; but an undercurrent could be felt, and raised evening voices from the officers' *basha* across the way frequently hinted at quarrels carefully suppressed during the daytime. The availability to officers of a monthly ration of liquor did not ease tensions. Enlisted men got only a case of 3.2 beer, little better than the "soapsuds" we called it, but an officer's allotment included a fifth or two of whiskey, and some traded cigarettes and candy bars for more. Captain Melvin, one of the entomologists, had been in the CBI far too long, endured bad weather and recurrent fevers oftener than was desirable for any man; and he often took on enough alcohol to release his exhaustion and anger and especially his contempt for Colonel Mackie's credentials as an epidemiologist, once going so far as to shout, so loudly we heard every syllable clearly in our own quarters, that Mackie was "nothing but a Park Avenue gynecologist who got his jollies tickling the clits of rich dowagers." Hotter words yet followed, a court-martial was mentioned and the dispute only ended when Melvin was sent home.

Hostilities between enlisted cliques simmered but never reached that point; and in fact, Ira Singer excepted (he was by then working in a field hospital in China), I made my best army friends in the Typhus Commission, establishing comradeships that, unlike most bonds formed in wartime, have proved lifelong. Captain Bob Austrian—though till long after the war I never called him anything but "Captain"—was the first. Already a physician, perhaps ten years older than I, he was the son of a distinguished Baltimore internist, Dr. Charles Austrian, who was on the faculty of the Johns Hopkins School of Medicine, from which Bob himself had graduated in 1940, only a year or so later to take a commission in the Medical Corps and his place in the "Hopkins unit," the 18th General Hospital, and go overseas with it to Fiji, then India and at last to the Typhus Commission. All that was impressive enough, but what endeared him to me from our first meeting was his immense warmth, friendliness and obvious absorption in the intellectual problems scrub typhus posed. He was not only very bright, which most doctors are, but very curious, which many are not, and his curiosity covered a broad spectrum of cultural interests apart from medicine: he knew a lot about music, art and books, in all of which he encouraged my rising interest. When I told him I hadn't yet had calculus he offered at once to tutor me and we ordered a textbook and course outline from the army's educational program—though in the end I proved to be mathematically ineducable. Once, when I came into the lab whistling an old Artie Shaw arrangement, he looked up and said, "Where'd you learn to modulate that trickily?" "What's 'modulate'?" I asked, and got a short seminar in Bach, Mozart and Bix Beiderbecke. He liked me to drive him, as I have told, despite my mooniness, and on those afternoon excursions we talked about everything, much more to my benefit, I daresay, than his. The prospect of my attending Johns Hopkins after the war, which my father had arranged, pleased him, for he had been a Hopkins undergraduate too. Years later he did medical research at the Rockefeller Institute and then finally as professor of research medicine at the University of Pennsylvania

Medical School, capping his career by winning the Lasker Award for his development of a successful vaccine against pneumonia. To his olive complexion and raven-black hair he added deep, dark eyes that could switch from fraternal amusement to disappointed censure in an instant, both of which I often provoked; and his willingness to befriend and teach and encourage a naive Southern boy still awkwardly finding himself was one of the happiest pieces of good fortune to befall me during World War II.

My other close friends were my tent mates. Gene Hughes, with whom I'd gone to work the Ledo outbreak, was my daily laboratory companion as well, and from him I learned a lot about gerbils, animal autopsies, staining *Rickettsiae* slides, roaming the bush and looking for precious stones, in the knowledge of all of which he'd managed, without the benefit of textbooks or mentors, to make himself proficient. But I valued him for more than his quirky expertise in the odd corners of learning. At thirty he was the most seasoned of our circle, full of opinions but patient and able at times of crisis to set impulse aside while reason and experience struggled to express themselves; and in addition he was unfailingly good-humored under circumstances that were cumulatively wearing and often ominous.

Clegg and Kailey were of my own age, give or take a few months, and the three of us had grown up at the same time and in similar ways. Richard Marshall Clegg—"Caroline" to everyone—came, as I did, from North Carolina, though in his case the accent and manner were more pronounced. He had grown up only thirty miles from Winston-Salem, in Greensboro, and we belonged to identical high-school classes in rival football towns, but we had never met before the Typhus Commission brought us together. He was tall and slender, built like a basketball player, wore glasses; and his invariable demeanor was one of great gentleness, for he smiled easily, spoke softly and was almost impossible to arouse from his mild, benevolent view of the world. His courage was immense, however, perhaps the greatest of anyone working in scrub typhus: he was in entomology and spent most days striding the tall grass, where mites attached themselves to his tightly tucked-in trousers; back at the lab he swept them into glassware for microscopic examination and classification, though at any time a mite, or several, could have escaped and bitten him, possibly fatally.

Ross Kailey—mysteriously but universally called "Frogg"—could never have been mistaken for a basketballer, but was a giant: at six-five or -six, with shoulders and torso to match, he looked instead like Norman Rockwell's idea of a fullback, though he gave no evidence of having played football or even being interested in it. His hands and feet were equally huge, and he was powerful in the way only very large, very sinewy men can be; but in fact he was the outfit's clown, given to wearing a battered civilian porkpie hat, sent from home, that made him look like Denny Dimwit from the comics, given to bad jokes and offhand jests—we were in the "long haul for the short dough," he'd say, "a dollar a day and try to collect it." He ran the TyCom maintenance crew, a grab-bag assortment of Kachins from the next village, and through their headman, a wrinkled old-timer whom he called "Goldie," he saw to it that repairs were made, the Lister bags filled daily with sterilized drinking water, supplies brought in for the kitchen, mail fetched and a thousand other odds and ends done. He may have been the ablest scrounger in Burma, or even in the army, and eventually got us, besides the red parachute, a shortwave radio and a turntable for playing records. But in one instance his "liberations" failed him: when his ax slipped one day and made a deep cut in his boot, nearly cutting his foot as well, he discovered his foot was so large no boot or shoe of his size could be had in the CBI, and he had to wait months while a replacement pair was shipped from the States. It was, he liked to say, an "axident."

XXI

Jungle is oppressive in any season—dark, humid, silent except for the menacing but invariably unexpected screams of invisible birds and beasts skulking in the tangled undergrowth—and during the rains brought annually by the Asian monsoon it is suffocating. It rained frequently most of that winter and spring, but the serious rains of 1945 began a few weeks after V-E Day and continued with little relief until the end of August. By then, though none of us fully understood what was happening to us, most members of the U.S.A. Typhus Commission were half mad. We'd been in the jungles of Burma too long.

The daily round by which we lived and worked would hardly have suggested so. Though the outfit was larger and our labs and quarters were an improvement on the old site down the hill, the routine was as short and no more urgent than it had been. The casualness of our military demands and customs would have shocked a West Pointer—or a V.M.I. alumnus, for that matter—and beyond living in enlisted barracks and addressing officers by their ranks we dressed and acted so informally an outsider would have had difficulty telling us apart. The food was as good as ever, and officers and men ate the same daily fare together. Free time was plentiful, and as the war wound down recreational opportunities increased. Each month brought a fresh assortment of the splendid paperbacks in the Armed Services Editions, so insatiable readers enjoyed a supply of books perpetually—often surprisingly—replenished: one remarkable thick volume, a dual selection, combined *Huckleberry Finn* and *The Ambassadors*, thus offering young American soldiers their national literature's most innocent and most sophisticated novels between two flimsy covers.

There were other relaxations. We had sixteen-millimeter prints of new Hollywood movies two or three nights a week, projected onto a sheet by dutiful Bob Belcher, who though only a sergeant was a graduate entomologist in the daytime; the reels often slipped, blurring the picture and sending the soundtrack into a whine, and more than one movie had to carry over a night when a downpour interrupted its initial screening, but we grew used to such minor annoyances, meanwhile reveling in Bogart and Bacall, Rathbone and Bruce, Karloff and Lugosi, Grable and Payne, all of whom appeared again and again in identical pairings in nearly identical roles in wholly identical pictures. Now and then a "major" film turned up—*Laura, To Have and Have Not, The Clock*, an underrated bio-pic of George Gershwin unsurprisingly entitled *Rhapsody in Blue*—and we watched it over and over, loudly demanding that patient Bob Belcher rewind the reels and show it a second time, maybe a third.

Sports proved more difficult. The rugged terrain precluded football, baseball and basketball, but a volleyball court of sorts was laid out between buildings and daily games became a feature of any afternoon free of rain. Gene Hughes, Caroline Clegg and I, all tennis players in better days, built a makeshift badminton court nearby when we heard badminton equipment was available from Special Services in Myitkyina. This looked promising and through Frogg Kailey we made a requisition. The result was more generous than anyone could have anticipated: the next week a six-by-six supply truck backed up and dumped our equipment—two nets without posts, a single tube of birds and a thousand shiny new badminton racquets, the best America made. The driver offered no explanation and refused to take the spares back, and in the end the three of us, the only TyCom soldiers interested in playing, took to smashing our racquets after bad shots and fetching fresh ones in their place, though we barely decreased the supply before leaving Burma.

Mail, as with all soldiers in most of the wars we

know of, was a constant preoccupation. It was literally the lifeline by which we maintained our connection with what was for us the world of reality and sanity from which to draw what faith we could still muster in human decency. It worked both ways: it was as crucial to write letters home as to get them in return, for like the monthly shoebox packages of cookies and snapshots and toothpaste our families could send us, letters, even when they came in the miniature, single-page, photographically reproduced form of "V-Mail," were tangible proof that despite our fears we had not lost our families and sweethearts and friends. I was a tireless correspondent, as all of us were, pouring out page upon page night after night to my parents, my sister, Nancy, pals in Europe and the South Pacific, Freddy Speas, gravely ill with leukemia but stubbornly sticking to his classes in medical school; and all of them gave back as generously as they got, even the registrar at Johns Hopkins, Irene Davis, through whose good offices my father had effected my transfer as and when the war was over. Our letters home were censored by TyCom officers; letters to us were not, the assumption being, I suppose, that they had no military secrets to spill though we did—a manifest absurdity at which we sneered. My mother wrote me three or four times a week in her elegant hand and flawless prose, long flowing letters giving me the neighborhood news and gossip, whom she'd seen, who'd asked about me after church, what she was reading, doing, thinking. Though briefer, my father's letters, typed by him at his office, were, in their charm and affectionate tone and invariably reversed *e*'s and *i*'s, as distinctive as hers. Down the block Grady Southern's father, who could remember his own loneliness in France in 1918, began putting together a monthly neighborhood newsletter of which he typed multiple onionskin copies himself to mail to all of us who'd grown up together, never failing to remind everyone that "old J. P."—I, who needed no reminder—was the farthest away of us all: farther than Grady, in Hawaii, farther than Tommy Speas, in France and Belgium, farther even than Bob Stevenson and Nick Dimling, who were in POW camps in Germany and Poland, respectively. But Nancy's letters were the most precious, the thread linking me to the girl who, in my imagination, grew prettier, blonder, bluer-eyed and wiser daily as I sank, like everyone around me, into the rice paddies and quagmires of the Asian rain forest. People who smile at adolescent love have forgotten its intensity and poignancy.

Yet for all our small amenities we were unhappy men—or at least I was, in a time when open admission of one's blues and anxieties and formless nighttime dreads was discouraged by the universal code of masculine "strength." I have pondered those gloomy last days of the war for many years but found no single explanation. Surely part was the abominable weather: for more than fifty consecutive days it rained in torrents most of the day and night, flooding trails and some roads out of existence, filling the drainage ditches nearly to overflowing, keeping T-shirts, khakis, fatigues, socks, skivvies and boots perpetually damp and mildewed, turning the grounds and paths between TyCom buildings into a viscous mud that never dried; and between showers the tropical sun came out and brought clouds of steam from trees and mud and scorched faces and arms with its merciless glare. Coming hard upon the stifling humidity and closeness of the jungle itself, the rains were depressing and inescapable.

Loneliness was another cause. Mail held us to our established ties and affections, but as the months became a year, then more, the ties seemed increasingly fragile, the people we loved impossibly distant, America itself impossibly innocent; and we had no prospect of release to which we could look forward, for World War II inductions were for the proverbial "duration plus six months," the point at which duration ended being left carefully undefined. The army would learn better later, forced by Vietnam to recognize that men serving overseas tours become emotionally saturated and deepeningly depressed, even psychotic, if denied the certainty that on a specific date the tour will end. But that would be too late for us. What we bitched about loudly and endlessly was literally, hopelessly true. We'd been away too long, in the CBI too long, in the jungle, without relief, too long. As the saying put it, we were "nervous in the service."

An added but unarticulated discontent was that the research had become static, that the Typhus Commission had lost its steam. I was too inexperienced to grasp this directly, but in the unaltering laboratory routine I could sense, at least, that nothing was going forward: beyond transferring rickettsial strains from one set of gerbils to the next we did little, and there was nothing to suggest that we were learning—or had learned—anything about scrub typhus not known long since. But Gene Hughes and I, close to some of the younger officers with whom we worked and talked intimately, picked up more: that ugly differences between the professional staff, scientific as well as personal, were worsening; more, that Colonel Mackie, who boasted a lot about our similarity to the Yellow Fever Commission led in Cuba at the turn of the century by Walter Reed, to whom he obviously hoped to be compared, was at the heart of it; and that Mackie's vanity and ambition, extraordinary even in a war that had already produced Douglas MacArthur and George Patton, were the crux of the contention. For some of the scientists his lust for fame as a great figure in the history of tropical disease, not to mention his schemes for winning it, were fatally undermining the real purpose of the Typhus Commission, which was simply, impersonally to advance medical knowledge, and they seemed increasingly unbuttoned in showing their rancor.

All of this shook my confidence in what we were doing, though none of it was ever perfectly clear, a cluster of scowls, glares, mutterings and asides, ambiguities beyond the only slowly developing psychological understanding of a boy who'd seen few quarrels more serious than the juvenile disputes of the playground or ballfield. But for still another source of my unhappiness

I could point to no one but myself. For reasons still mysterious to me—carelessness? stupidity? mere innocence?—I became the victim of a series of misadventures, all absurd and two nearly fatal. The first, a few days after I joined the Typhus Commission, was the result of an effort to protect me from scrub typhus. Scientists at Walter Reed Hospital in Washington had developed an experimental vaccine they hoped would be effective against possible infection with the disease we were investigating—a frequent and frequently mortal occurrence amongst rickettsial workers—and giving it to TyCom staffers had become routine, the hope being that it would produce an immunity not only for them but, eventually, for everyone in a risky area. Captain Austrian duly stuck my arm and neither of us thought more about it. The lunch bell sounded. Within ten minutes my ears began to roar; I could feel my lips swelling and from across the table Frogg noticed my outer ears reddening and beginning to thicken. Bob Austrian looked up from the officers' table and leaped suddenly to his feet. "Come on," he said, "We're going in to Myitkyina."

"What's wrong?"

"You're having an allergic reaction."

"Allergic to what?"

"The typhus shot," he said. "Let's *go*."

I was in the hospital—the 18th General Hospital, from which I'd transferred to the Typhus Commission—ten days. By the time we got there my heart rate had risen to one hundred and thirty and I was covered with welts. They pumped me full of adrenalin and put me to bed. In an hour or two my pulse was pounding again and the welts had returned. My face was covered; my chest and belly were covered; the soles of my feet were covered and itched beyond control. A nurse gave me more adrenalin. Old friends came in to scratch my feet.

It lasted a week, and it took a day or two more to get me steady again. It was a ludicrous event but I learned later that medically it was a dangerous one; and I did not much like the unromantic notion of a wartime death from, of all things, hives. Less comical was the realization that I could get no more shots and would thus be deprived of what possible protection army medicine offered. The more I pondered the hazard the more frightened I got.

A few weeks later, while helping a TyCom soldier named Ted Kocot string the frame of his cot with long strips of rubber cut from an old inner tube, the aim being to fashion a set of rudimentary bedsprings, the head-bar slipped, the rubber strips projected it my way like a giant slingshot and it hit me across the right hand, smashing my index finger across the third joint. It was off to the 18th General Hospital again for stitches and a splint; the finger healed slowly, the knuckle throbbed night and day and when the swelling subsided at last the finger was crooked and stiff. "Just adhesions," Bob Austrian assured me. No doubt, but forty-five years afterward it is still crooked, still stiff, and it throbs in cold weather.

My third accident was a nightmare that has never left me. One afternoon Frogg, Gene and I drove up into the hills toward Sumprabum to shoot at crows. On the way back we decided to cut through the jungle and follow a back trail into the Typhus Commission. A couple of miles in, however, we found the way blocked by a swollen stream that in drier weather we could ford. Frogg backed up and turned. I jumped out. "You two go on in the regular way," I said. "I'll go upstream a ways and cross where it's narrower, then walk in."

It was a foolhardy blunder—it is never wise to go into jungle alone; but we were scarcely a mile from camp and they didn't argue. I listened as the sound of the jeep fell away, then wheeled and started into the clearing. Toward the far end something moved suddenly, and as I snapped down my carbine an apparition burst toward me perhaps a hundred feet away.

I could not tell whether he was a Chinese or a Japanese deserter, though the bush was full of both; but his ragged, dirty khaki shirt and trousers were clearly what was left of a uniform, and he was carrying some sort of rifle and he was pointing it at me as he ran. It was a crazy parody of a banzai charge, but his unshaven cheeks and staring eyes told me in the single flashing glimpse I got of him that he was even more alone than I and altogether as scared. I toppled into a roll to my right, straight out of basic training though it was reflexive rather than planned, and it saved my life. He fired as he neared, a shot from below the waist, and I heard the round whish past; but he'd missed, and I fired too, missing too at nearly point-blank range—so much for either's marksmanship—and he sped past, giving me a second glimpse of his terrified expression. I rolled on and turned again and saw the last of him, a foot vanishing into the greenery. Then he fired again and I felt an instant's scorching pain at my left shoulder blade. Suddenly everything went perfectly quiet. The undergrowth fell still. The whole thing may have lasted as much as ten seconds.

I lay motionless. I was shaking uncontrollably, and though I thought he was gone I was uncertain. After a minute or two I got to one knee, and when nothing happened I stood. I saw no one. I headed for the Irrawaddy.

It proved difficult. The bush was thick, but I knew if I found the river I could follow the bank downstream till I reached the Typhus Commission; besides, it was in the opposite direction from my Oriental antagonist, whoever and whatever he was. I swung my carbine before me a few times to clear my way; twice I had to fling myself facedown against the vines to get through. But at last the sky brightened and a moment later I was at river's edge. I ripped off my T-shirt and jumped into the shallow water. A mile away, where the Irrawaddy curved back toward me, I spied the top of a TyCom tent. I got out of the water, sat down on the bank and began to cry.

The scorch on my back proved to be a scratch, probably a glancing wound from another poor shot, no worse than the hundreds of scratches I'd got playing football and baseball as a boy. It had stopped seeping. Presently I stood and started home. I had to swim the swollen stream where it entered the river, but after those ten seconds in the clearing it was nothing. When I got to camp everyone was at chow. I took off the rest of my clothes, jumped into the water, then dressed again and went up the hill to tell them what had happened. No one had missed me; they laughed at my story. I could scarcely believe it myself. When I went to bed I realized I'd lost my silver V.M.I ring. Next morning I spotted it at the bottom of the river and dove to fetch it—proof, to me at least, that I hadn't imagined it all.

xxii

We got the news of Hiroshima through the bulky, "portable" shortwave radio, painted army o.d., on the table in our room. The first flash came over Armed Forces Radio from Delhi; we tried at once to switch to Tokyo Rose, but Japan, usually the strongest and most dependable broadcast signal we got, had gone off the air, and when we returned to the Delhi report it seemed, like almost all American propaganda, flat, incomplete and cryptic. But it hardly mattered. Anyone in science—anyone, in fact, who'd had even the most rudimentary high-school chemistry or physics—knew what it meant. Unless Japan had an "A-bomb" too, as the news was already nicknaming it, the war was over. The bombing of Nagasaki a few days later meant they had no A-bomb.

We were neither elated nor downcast by the news. The fact that a single bomb had destroyed an entire city and that it had killed so many people in a single explosion did not surprise us—we understood in a flash what the power of released nuclear energy must be. Nor did it sadden us or fill us with guilt—Japan had started the war and waged it with extraordinary ferocity and brutality, and, besides, by now we were accustomed to death and destruction. In retrospect it seems we took it too casually; but like exhausted men everywhere we'd grown not so much hardened and cynical as numb and dull, perhaps dull-witted. What Hiroshima and Nagasaki mostly meant was that we were going home, a possibility many of us, though never quite saying so, had come to doubt.

The rains fell incessantly that week, bringing almost everything to a halt; but the ultimate news that the Japs had surrendered, and surrendered unconditionally, as the Allies had demanded, came before dawn and before we'd turned on the radio, so we first heard it when what sounded like a shotgun fired outside. We staggered out to find Captain Austrian stomping almost naked through the rain and mud, shotgun raised to fire again, yelling so loudly we could hear him over the downpour, "It's over! It's over!" No one went to the labs all day, and in the early afternoon, fairly drunk himself, Bob Austrian came over and, violating army regulations, customs and probably good sense, ceremoniously deposited an unopened bottle of Scotch on our table. It was generous; it was typical; and soon we four were as drunk as KA pledges at a University of Virginia mixer.

The morning after brought fresh questions: how soon would we go home? would we go together? and by what priorities would the army determine the order of our demobilization? Colonel Mackie had flamboyantly and repeatedly promised to take the Typhus Commission back as a unit; but he was off on another mysterious trip to Washington and no one left behind had the authority to accomplish that. Meanwhile the long-termers and middle-agers and the men with wives and children could do little but bite their nails while the army decided, and the rest of us, mostly youngsters, got, we hoped, in line. The only thing that seemed certain was that we wouldn't be invading Japan.

Work stalled. The American presence in Myitkyina began to thin. We got orders to destroy surplus government property and did, dumping tons of tires, spare parts and even entire vehicles in the Irrawaddy to the astonishment of watching Kachins, who in their poverty might well have had use for them; they got the same shock watching us smash new wristwatches on railroad tracks, burn box after box of unopened, unused sports equipment, including nearly a thousand badminton racquets, and hurl hundreds of phonograph records into the river—they made wonderful if premature and wholly wasteful Frisbees. All of this was to prevent United States property from falling into "foreign hands," a point whose delicacy the friendly Kachins, many of whom had helped the army to liberate their country and whose country it was, after all, must have found it difficult to appreciate. Downriver a few miles the quartermasters were disposing of warehouses of canned and dried food the same way. It was my first experience of the arrogant imperialism in which the United States would surpass the more benign imperialism of the British in coming years.

Presently the rules for returning American servicemen to the States came down: a system in which, from his official record, every soldier, sailor and marine received "points" based upon the length of his service, the length of his stint overseas, the number of his dependents and the decorations he had won, all totaled as of V-J Day and unalterable thereafter. It sounded as fair and as consistent with the realities of wartime service as an armed force of sixteen million could devise, for it ignored rank and the nature of service, which could vary with an extraordinary range of circumstances, and favored those who'd served the longest and, in the case of husbands and fathers, often sacrificed the most. What it failed to acknowledge, what it took us awhile to see, was distance from the States and the unhappy truth that it would be easier and thus faster to return troops from Europe, which was closer, and the South Pacific, which was full of American ships, than from India and Burma, which were literally half the world away. When in the months that followed many of us boasting points in the sixties, fifties and forties learned that soldiers were going home from

Shanghai with twenty points or fewer it was an unpleasant surprise.

Points at least offered certainty of sorts. But for us an overriding doubt remained: what would become of the Typhus Commission, hence what would become of us? No word came from Mackie, but suddenly the officers began to disappear, flying out of Myitkyina and, via Ledo, Delhi, Cairo and points west, eventually to Washington. Yet no explanation was extended us; they simply *went*, while we remained. Dismantlement of the labs proceeded. We were down to a skeleton crew, but without illumination, let alone orders.

Then, as mysteriously as the officers had vanished, we enlisted men were ordered back to India, where, at Headquarters Company, Ledo Area Command, we were transferred to the 971st QM Supply Detachment. Quartermasters? A "supply detachment"? We were medics, technicians; and anyway no such organization existed. We were also, we suddenly realized, high and dry and not returning to the States with the Typhus Commission to "get the credit" Mackie had said we deserved.

We went back by small convoy over the Ledo Road, now all but abandoned and beginning, where it wasn't already overgrown, to wash away. By now I was a buck sergeant, a three-striper, and though not yet the ranking sergeant of the party I was ranking enough that when the convoy got divided at a swollen stream I had to take charge of the forward section, reaching Ledo a day ahead of the rest. At Headquarters Company the sergeant major handed me a stack of personnel folders. "Trick or treat," he said, then grinned wickedly.

"Meaning what?"

"Read 'em and weep."

I took the folders to the far side of the orderly tent and sat down to flip through them. The first was that of a busted corporal doing time in the Ledo stockade for theft. The second was for a PFC, also busted, confined for going over the hill in Bombay. The third made my blood run cold: it was for a soldier serving a long sentence for beating an MP nearly to death with the MP's billy. I went through the rest at a dash; all thirty were the files of yardbirds, army inmates jailed for a range of crimes all serious enough to warrant extended imprisonment. I looked up.

"Rough lot, all right," the sergeant major said, his voice now sympathetic. "But there's more."

"How can there be?"

"You've got them. They're your new outfit, and they arrive tomorrow . . . "

"And?"

"You ain't asked me what you're gonna do," he said. "You and the rest of your guys will be the non-com cadre for the yardbirds. And what you're gonna do is dig up all the American graves in India and Burma."

The yardbirds duly arrived, presumably chastened and motivated by a promise of army discharge at least less than dishonorable if they behaved and performed well as gravediggers, and we took up quarters at the old

69th General Hospital, now as abandoned as almost everything else in Ledo, where we got an old ward, an orderly room where the dental clinic had been and mess assignment with a neighboring truck company unaccountably left behind when everyone else was leaving. A day or two later we got our commanding and only officer—our "company commander," though we were not a company and he could not have commanded a latrine detail—a pink-faced second lieutenant fresh out of OCS who'd been in the army less than six months, had just reached the CBI and just got the happy news that his wife had borne them twin girls. He was as hopelessly unseasoned as a boy scout, and it seemed a shame to have to give him the sorry tidings that his first command were who they were and would have to do what they would. But he had the animal sense to know when he was in over his head, and he smiled weakly and said, "Well, they told us in OCS when in doubt let the sergeants run the army. So you guys go ahead, and"—his smile now fading—"I'll be the front guy."

Our first job was the Ledo cemetery, a big one, the army's plan being to remove all military remains throughout the theater to a single graveyard in Calcutta, from which, if the families requested it, they could in turn be shipped to the States for reburial at home. After the first day's exhumations it became clear that this was a poor plan, and that it would be an even poorer plan if survivors opened the caskets to have a last look at Jack, Jim or Buddy. The army's incessant propaganda, spread through a hundred war movies, had encouraged the widespread delusion that most soldiers die cleanly, smiling bravely to the last, from wounds in the shoulders or legs, though in fact most die from wounds or infections that leave their bodies mangled, misshapen or disfigured; and the corpses we dug up—shot, crushed, disemboweled, burned, flayed, in one case hanged by the thick black neck for a murder—were invariably in wretched states of decomposition that would have shaken the most hardened fan of horror movies and perhaps struck the ultimate blow to parents, wives and sweethearts already stricken by loss. The sweet smell of decayed flesh alone was sickening and so powerful it stuck to our nostrils and uniforms despite repeated showers and launderings.

It was filthy, disgusting and eventually, as we all discovered, depressing work that none of us wanted to do, but for the time being, no doubt still bearing fresh memories of the equally grim horrors of the stockade, the yardbirds lay low; and we had help. Two companies of Indian labor troops, from Travancore, did the hard digging, following records and charts kept by Army Graves Registration. But when they hit the original caskets they stepped aside, unwilling to handle the dead, whose bodies, by custom, they more sensibly burned. At that point a couple of us dropped into the hole, broke open the side of the box, pulled out the corpse and handed it up; there others wrapped it in a fresh shelter half, tied it and its accompanying dog tag to a litter and hauled the litter to a waiting truck, where still others of our merry crew placed it in a new wooden casket, screwed down the lid, affixed the dog tag to the top and stowed the casket in the truck. When the truck was full it drove its load to the airstrip to be placed inside a C-47; when the C-47 was full it flew its cargo to Calcutta and the caskets were delivered into other hands for reburial there. The procedure was arduous, but the army had a system, which it often didn't, and the system made sense, which it rarely did; and the records were perfect if the bodies weren't.

When we'd finished Ledo we did nearby Chabua, Dibrugarh, Digboi and Tinsukia, all until recently the sites of airstrips that had been the bases for flying the Hump; then we moved on to Shingbwiyang, well down the Ledo Road, where the army had started a graveyard on the spot where the first infantryman had fallen during the reinvasion of Burma nearly two years before. That was his misfortune; ours was that he had fallen at the crest of a hill so steep it took more than two hundred wooden steps cut into the slope to reach the top—while the trucks remained below. The earliest remains, buried unwrapped in bare earth, were by now skeletons and light, but the rest, soggy from their caskets, were unbelievably heavy for even four men to lug clumsily downhill. The yardbirds began to grumble, and several contrived to get drunk and surly on rice wine bought or stolen in the village.

More serious trouble erupted in Myitkyina, the last graveyard we had to exhume along the upper rim of the CBI. I flew down a few days later than the rest, staying in Ledo to close out our paperwork, and arrived to find the lieutenant wringing his hands. The steady withdrawal of troops had left Myitkyina a ghost town, actually the ghost of a ghost from its prewar size, shape and make-up, and all that remained was a handful of soldiers liquidating the little still visible of the American presence in a few *bashas* and tents clustered about the old residency. The exodus and the resulting absence of authority had left Myitkyina effectively an open town; deserters from the Chinese armies had moved from the surrounding hills and jungles into the area around the bazaar to become the virtual rulers; and in this vacuum one of our yardbirds had sold the lieutenant's jeep to a bandit.

This was no trifle. The jeep was army property the army wished to destroy in its own way; the lieutenant was responsible for it and selling it to anyone, let alone a Chinese bandit, was a major military crime. Tension was already so high we'd mounted a perimeter, .30-calibre machine gun included, around the compound. The bandit drove past frequently, glaring hard. I talked the yardbird out of his roll of bills by telling him what a fix he was in and promising, altogether illegally, to drop the matter if we got the jeep back. Then the lieutenant and I decided to go to the bazaar and repurchase his jeep.

We were spared what could have been a risky trip. The Chinese bandit—a swarthy, stocky fellow wearing a brace of ammo belts across his chest like the Mexican bandit in *The Treasure of the Sierra Madre* a few years later—sought us out. He was having trouble with the jeep. It sputtered and missed and stalled. The lieutenant held up the money and said we'd swap and forget. The bandit looked at him, at me, at the machine gun beside the door. His hostility was palpable as he fingered the army .45-calibre Colt automatic, presumably also recent American property, at his waist. The moment was dangerous. But then, slowly, he began to nod, then smile, then shrugged and took the money. When he'd gone the lieutenant looked down and saw he'd wet his khakis.

The yardbirds gave us another scare two days later when we flew out. Twilight was falling before the last casket had been exhumed and put aboard. After ten minutes in the air one of the yardbirds' big duffel bags began to move. When he opened it a little brown Kachin girl, a teenager, popped out like a chorus girl from a cake. I told the crew chief, who said, "Holy shit," and went to tell the pilot. The C-47 banked suddenly, turning back to Myitkyina. By the time we'd dumped the girl and taken off again the darkness was complete. Upon landing at Chabua we felt the right wing scrape the concrete.

xxiii

By the time we reached Calcutta, India's largest city and thereafter the headquarters of the 971st's gravedigging operation, I was experiencing personal nightly disturbances for which, by the conventional wisdom of the time, there was no medical explanation. Since leaving Myitkyina I'd been overwhelmed by images of destruction, not surprisingly after what I'd seen there and in Bhamo, Lashio and Mandalay, and found them inescapable. To the nightmares they produced was now added the malady of bolting upright nearly every night from a deep sleep, waking as I did, breath short, heart pounding, clear images of death and the dead passing before my eyes as my heart gradually slowed. I saw the corpses we were unearthing in all their stages of decay;

closer yet, I saw the faces of friends recently dead—Jim Delery, who'd tried to teach me bridge on the long voyage to India, killed in China; Klemasakis, TyCom's great cook, lost when the plane taking him home from Burma crashed into a mountainside in the Naga Hills. Gravedigging was an unrelievedly gruesome task, which might have explained some of it, and losing friends and companions is an inevitable feature of war; but my physical reaction was frightening. In the Typhus Commission I'd lived in perpetual fear that without the vaccination presumably protecting the rest I'd contract scrub typhus; but the fear had seemed under firm control, a mere background anxiety. Now, in the relative safety of Calcutta, everything seemed to be backing up. At the dispensary a bored doctor eager to get home looked me over, at my insistence listening to my heart because of its nighttime pounding, and assured me offhandedly that I was in fine shape; and when I told him about the yardbirds and the job he shrugged, the universal army reaction to any problem. But despite his soothing words I was not soothed. Two decades later I would revisit my situation in *The Dirty Dozen*, but with the important difference that our enterprise was no movie and I was no Lee Marvin. The widespread complaints of Vietnam veterans also reminded me that no diagnosis as sympathetic as "posttraumatic stress" existed in the medical thought of World War II. Emotions were sissy, and a soldier so weak as to feel them should keep it to himself.

Numbing oneself to what one saw and felt thus

became a way of surviving and of saving one's sanity. Calcutta helped. To many before and after me it was and is an obscene and intolerable case of social depravity, the "city of dreadful night," as Kipling called it, the world's worst urban failure; and certainly the evidence of its overcrowding and poverty was inescapable. Beggars were everywhere. The horribly crippled victims of malnutrition and congenital and tropical disease thronged the most fashionable streets. The *bustees* of the homeless and destitute—makeshift shantytowns of rotten wood and cardboard often leaning against the rear walls of stolid buildings in the central commercial area—could be spied down alleyways. Smoke from the *ghats* where the daily dead were ritually burned filled the air. Yet after more than a year of jungle Calcutta seemed charming, whether because it really was or because we'd become inured to suffering and would have been glad to be anywhere away from Burma I did not and do not know.

It had tremendous breadth and depth and vitality, in any case, a dramatic example of life flourishing in the midst of death. The great public buildings of its Victorian heyday as the capital of Britain's Indian empire still stood, simultaneously projecting power and beauty. Along the vast esplanade of Chowringhee Boulevard the fine hotels, restaurants, banks and "palaces" of the Raj emanated strength and elegance. Across the boulevard, almost as big as Hyde Park, the Maidan rolled on green and gracious, Calcutta's "lungs" and the playground on which Brits and rajahs and their entourages played tennis and cricket and downed cooling gimlets. Nearby were museums and galleries and fine shops, and against the far side, commanding the Hooghly River, the ramparted remains of Fort William, scene of the "Black Hole," were a reminder of the improbable empire put together, in the wake of that famous massacre, by freebooting adventurers like Job Carnock and Robert Clive and Warren Hastings.

Calcutta was exciting, had color and glamour and a rousing history, and a boy of twenty could ignore, if he chose, the ugly other side of its more dubious present. By early 1946 Gene, Frogg and Caroline had gone home on the strength of their accumulated points; but I made a few new friends amongst the other non-coms of neighboring outfits. The 971st was quartered and messed at Camp Knox, a little installation of Quonset huts in the southern suburb of Tollygunge originally built to house the crews of naval vessels temporarily berthed at the docks of the Hooghly. Other outfits, most nearly as small as ours, were quartered there too, sharing a single hut for their various orderly rooms and another, larger hut as a community dayroom; we played Ping-Pong there, and there was a record player and a stack of the red-labeled 78-RPM "Victrola" records manufactured in Calcutta on license from the American company; most were of popular swing bands and singers—Glenn Miller, Tommy Dorsey, Dinah Shore, Frank Sinatra, a fine rendition of "Let's Fall in Love" by Benny Goodman and Red Norvo that I was never able to run down after the war—all of whom seemed to be as popular in India as they were back home. I no longer went out on digs, having taken over the orderly room as acting first sergeant, and it was pleasant, once the morning report, sick list and other paperwork were done, to idle away most of the day reading or playing chess in the dayroom; but really the other orderly-room sergeants and I were awaiting midafternoon and an evening in downtown Calcutta.

Small units of the 971st, each led by a corporal or buck sergeant, flew out all over India and down the Arakan coast of Burma on the Bay of Bengal exhuming American dead in cemeteries often as small as three or four graves. Back in Calcutta the lieutenant and I booked their flights and arranged with the Graves Registration people for daily reburials in the growing Calcutta graveyard. But when that was done we were free for the day. I, at least, was nervously marking time as I neared the day when my forty-four points would put me on a troopship headed home. I was scarcely alone in that: everyone but the newest arrivals was counting the days—and trying to remain healthy and in one piece lest a last-minute illness or injury delay his departure.

One of us nearly always had a jeep at his disposal, and our custom was to drive in after three, leave the jeep at an army car park in the Maidan, then wander off to do each as he liked. I liked looking into the historic buildings of the Raj—the Governor's Palace, the great state office buildings of Dalhousie Square, Fort William, the Victoria Memorial near the south end of the Maidan—for though the seat of power had long since shifted to Delhi one still felt the presence of such great British rulers as Canning and Curson. I liked the museums too, and the bright Bengali paintings on display, and the movie houses showing British and American films with great panache; I soon grew used to the break between short subjects and features, when the audience moved to the mezzanine bar for a quick drink, as well as to the invariable ceremony of standing at the end of each showing for a brief film of the Union Jack waving serenely against a perfect blue sky while the soundtrack blared an invisible band's "God Save the King"; though I remained unsettled by the fact that smoking was permitted in theater seats. It was fun afterward to take tea at a nearby *patisserie* or to stroll an hour or so through the New Market, Calcutta's enormous roofed bazaar, perhaps then the biggest thing of its kind on earth, where one could buy anything from beautiful silk *saris* and shawls to ivory chessmen and figurines of tigers, lions and Mahatma Gandhi, not to mention battered secondhand copies, procured who knows where, of Bennett Cerf's own Modern Library. On one memorable occasion, after parking my jeep in the Maidan I saw an enormous crowd garbed in white break up a quarter of a mile away as a small figure ceased speaking, and learned later that the small figure was Gandhi himself; the crowd surged about me but was entirely friendly. But once the sun had set everyone went to Firpo's.

Like Rick's Café Americain in *Casablanca* Firpo's was one of those famous watering holes, found in every city of what is now called condescendingly the Third World, in which colonial administrators, soldiers, flashy women of presumably ambiguous virtue and assorted riffraff assembled after dark to conduct their affairs, whatever they were. A few Indian nabobs and their wives or doxies were admitted too if they were rich enough, but for the most part it was a white—though frequently shady—crowd. American servicemen got in automatically, unless intolerably drunk, even sergeants of twenty, for GI's were still, for British and Indians alike, the "damn fine Yanks" who'd kept them in the war; besides, we had cash. A big dining room served respectable customers on the street floor, but everyone else climbed the outside wooden staircase to the great covered verandah overlooking Chowringhee and the Maidan, which opened through French doors into a huge ballroom where across the dance floor from the round dining tables a little band of tuxedoed Indians tootled and hooted its often unsteady way through "Yes, We Have No Bananas," "The Music Goes 'Round and 'Round" and "A Nightingale Sang in Berkeley Square." Everything the ingenuity of the bartender could imagine was available to drink, but gin was king at Firpo's, as it was elsewhere in the East, usually with lime juice or quinine water, the medicinal properties of both being widely understood; it was important, of course, to drink only bottled mixes and to avoid ice, diseases like amoebic dysentery, typhoid and cholera still being endemic in India. Dinner around nine was usually excellent, though a GI accustomed to the dull fare of army mess halls could hardly have been a competent judge; and afterward it was common to dance, their husbands or lovers permitting, with the memsahibs.

The air was charged, for us at least, with sex. Few of us had so much as seen a woman, a nurse or two apart, for more than a year; most of us missed them and all of us were young. The mere presence of women was enough to set our starved libidos afire, and many of the women we saw at Firpo's were striking: the English roses with their blue eyes, fair hair and complexions of peaches and cream; their older counterparts, sisters, aunts and mothers, with their classic cheekbones, stately bearing and worldly, witty, frequently bawdy conversation; but above all the Anglo-Indians—half limey, half wog, as the vulgar put it—whose Asian dusky skin and eyes and raven hair combined with the perfect skin and height and confident posture of their Saxon forebears to give them the mysterious beauty personified on the screen by Merle Oberon, who was in fact an Anglo-Indian herself. In their *saris*, one shoulder bared, scented with sandalwood, they were so exotic they took the breath away. They knew it too and enjoyed the teasing games they played with us, though they were prudent and knew better than to form romantic alliances with GI's, who'd be gone tomorrow. With the boyish British officers who came to Firpo's they were clearly more serious: the lads of Sussex and

Dorset and Hampshire were better prospects for rescuing them from the ambivalence of half-breed life. We were merely fun—and endlessly tumescent.

We were that, and stuck with it, for the memsahibs—as we were properly careful to call them—knew where to stop; and we had either to quell our fantasies or satisfy them in the commercial but dangerous depths of Calcutta prostitution. Like poverty, whores were everywhere, as was disease, and more than one of my companions took the chance, usually in a dark alleyway off Chowringhee or Park Street only blocks from the elegance of Firpo's. I was too fastidious, or perhaps only too scared.

I was also right. One friend quickly developed a serious case of gonorrhea and my yardbirds fared even worse, sprouting several cases of syphilis, many cases of gonorrhea and a number of tropical sexual infections rarely seen among Americans. They tended also to wait too long to seek treatment, no doubt fearing punishment, and that tended in turn to reignite old infections as well as to protract their recoveries. Just before leaving India I learned from a sergeant major at area headquarters that despite its small size the 971st had the highest VD rate in the CBI, perhaps in the entire United States Army. I did not take the news to be a unit commendation.

It was typical, however. The yardbirds continued to be a nightmare for me, for though no one tried to sell any of our vehicles again they were all chronic misfits on whose behavior one didn't dare turn one's back. As long as they were separated by small gravedigging missions the non-coms could maintain a degree of control, but reassembled they immediately formed a critical mass. The worst havoc came on payday the week I got my orders. Payday was always a tense time in the army, often ending in quarrels and fights; soldiers were broke and the protocol rigid, demanding special dress and drill and empowering a pay officer to "redline"—withhold the pay of—anyone who got out of line or failed to satisfy his inspection. That last payday the yardbirds turned up drunk and dirty to a man, and some were hovering on violence. The danger was obvious and could have led to a riot. The finance officer who'd come to pay them was shooting suspicious looks up and down. At the last moment the lieutenant and I drew him aside and warned him what might happen if he redlined anyone. He waited a minute, then nodded, sat down and paid every disgusting one of them, curtly informing me afterward that they were "the sorriest fucking rabble" he'd "seen in four fucking years in the fucking army." I noticed the lieutenant fingering his .45 as the line passed, and I already knew I was fingering mine.

XXIV

As fascinating as I found Calcutta and as much as it had boosted my sinking spirits, I wanted desperately, like every other soldier, to go home. The war had been over for months; and to my exhaustion and disillusionment was now added the certain knowledge that my forty-four points would have returned me to the States and won me my army discharge long since were I in any other war zone. I wanted to see my family, see Nancy, see my friends, wanted to get back to college and resume my interrupted education; and I ached to know—what everyone serving in the CBI eventually realized—that we were at the end of the longest army line of all: the most distant theater, the poorest supplied, the most easily forgotten and neglected, now, at the end, the last to be brought home. That sense has pervaded CBI attitudes from General Joseph W. Stilwell at the top to the humblest private in the rearmost rank, and it continued to do so to the last man.

I had begun to fear I was going to be the last man myself, and my anxiety was not alleviated by the news that my boyhood best friends Tommy and Grady, neither of whom had been overseas any longer than I, were already out and back at college; nor was I cheered to learn from my mother that Colonel Mackie, the melodramatic commanding officer who after repeated promises to the contrary had left the Typhus Commission's enlisted men hanging out to dry, had been named the head of a new institute for tropical disease at Winston-Salem's Bowman Gray School of Medicine and was about to move into our neighborhood. Now it was clear what all those mysterious trips to Washington had really been about, as well as his overdone attention to me.

Time dragged as eligibility for departure neared my number of points, but I continued my custom of spending my evenings at Firpo's. Other opportunities arose. One afternoon, responding to an invitation posted at the Red Cross Burra Club on Dalhousie Square, I joined a group bused to the Calcutta home of Lady Ester, an elderly Englishwoman the rest of whose name I no longer recall; she looked like my grandmother—or like Queen Victoria, which is saying the same thing—and she gave us tea from a large tea-wagon in the drawing room of her "palace," a fantasy place behind a wall off Park Street with an immense rear garden, a sort of tamed jungle in which monkeys and ostriches paraded frantically while we GI's gawked. On another afternoon I talked the headquarters sergeant major into giving me a pass through an off-limits district so I could visit the Royal Institute of Tropical Medicine on Chittaranjan Boulevard; trailblazing research on malaria, cholera and filariasis had once been done there, and the doctors and technicians could not have welcomed me more warmly, but the labs and equipment were dusty and antiquated and the atmosphere was torpid, static, incurious. I watched tennis and cricket on the Maidan and strolled the New Market for the thirtieth or fortieth time. I lay in the grass by the Victoria Memorial and read Byron's poetry. I longed for a beautiful young memsahib to take pity and spirit me off to the unspeakable erotic delights of her own dusky "palace." I longed in vain.

The first week of March 1946, having missed the last troopship home by two points, I learned that my number had finally come up. I said goodbye without regrets to the lieutenant and the yardbirds, who for all I know may still be digging up graveyards in Asia, and reported, as ordered, to a staging area north of Calcutta called Dum Dum, where the Calcutta International Airport now is. It was the site at which the Great Mutiny had broken out in 1857, and we soldiers awaiting passage home, in army lingo the "next available T to the ZI" (transportation to the Zone of the Interior, in human terms), were housed in a moldy Muslim barracks that looked like an abandoned set for *The Charge of the Light Brigade*. There, having stopped taking atabrine to see what would happen, I came down with ferocious chills and fever but refused to go on sick call for fear I'd be hospitalized and further delay my return; the GI in the next bunk brought me tea, aspirin and what little food I could eat, and in a few days I was myself again, though I have suffered periodic bouts of malaria or something like it ever since.

At length we were ordered to ready ourselves and our gear, and late one night we were trucked to the docks of the Hooghly to board an American merchant ship, the *Marine Jumper*. The gangplank rose steeply, precisely opposite to the troopship that had brought me to India from California, and I took that to be a positive symbol. Things were looking up.

They were looking up in more ways than one. No longer needing to go dark at dusk, the *Jumper* ran lights at all hours and let us go on deck whenever we pleased. Other relaxations appeared. The food was as dreary as before, but another sergeant and I invited ourselves to the crew's mess and got away with it; there, meals were good, we were served seated and afterward we could use the room to read, play chess and listen to the radio, for which we thanked them by making fresh coffee at all hours. By the time we reached the States I had gone through *War and Peace, Crime and Punishment, Look Homeward, Angel* and *The Web and the Rock* and was just beginning *The History of Rome Hanks*, a wonderful novel about the American Civil War that deserved to be remembered longer than it was; I had bought all of them in cheap, secondhand copies in the New Market. The merchantmen let us try on their civvies; after so many years in uniform I found them light and loose and vaguely improper.

It was nonetheless a long voyage home, longer even than the tortuous zigzag of the *Pope* going over. We put in briefly at Singapore but were not allowed ashore, though from the deck we could see its famous coastal guns fixed to fire only toward the sea; and docked overnight in Manila, of which I formed no impression, though a friend woke me next morning in time to see Corregidor and the scorched mouth of Malinta Tunnel slip past as we sped from the bay. Both were forlorn reminders of the terrible defeats the United States and Britain had suffered in the opening days of the war on Japan, and they left me—accompanied by Tolstoy, Dostoevski and Wolfe, none of them cheerful writers—in pensive mood.

I had much to ponder. Young and still unformed though I was, I could not help but realize that I was nearing the end of a crucial period of my life and that I would be fundamentally and permanently affected by the experience. I read and walked and read and walked, finding in Tolstoy a rich perception of war and its follies and their meaning for all who suffer them. But Napoleon's invasion of Russia was not like Hitler's, no matter how diligently the publisher of my copy of *War and Peace* sought in an inserted brochure to stress the similarity, nor was the Napoleonic world much like the world totalitarianism had created—and my generation had been sent to destroy. War in that earlier time had been brutal, and warfare had certainly changed the political landscape, but by the standard of the twentieth century it had been simple: fought by limited numbers of men for limited aims against limited areas with weapons of drastically limited firepower; our war had been global, in the end affecting every continent, and it had been waged by unimaginable millions of warriors and civilians to win the absolute submission of their enemies with weapons of almost unimaginable destructiveness, at its end bringing to birth the most destructive weapon of all. More than sixteen million of those who fought World War II were Americans, and I was one of them; and I sought determinedly to explain to myself what doing so had meant.

Some of my experience had been good, I knew. I had been lucky, for the most part, in finding the branch and drawing or seeking the assignments I'd got; I had seen a lot and learned a lot that presumably would be valuable if I pursued, as I still believed I would, the study of medicine. I had escaped wounds, malnutrition or serious injury; I'd been fit and stayed fit, despite occasional reverses, and could thank my stars for my youth and condition. I had made friends I would keep for a lifetime. I had seen the world. I had grown. Best of all, perhaps, I had been part of an experience that, choose it or not, dwarfed all merely personal aspirations or fears; I had been present when the challenge came and I had met it. In the simple but genuine formulation of the day, I had served my country, which was to say that I had served the society that had nurtured and protected me, and I was deeply proud to have done so.

In those respects I was fortunate and knew it. But nothing in war is wholly good, and much that I had seen and experienced left me shaken. The corruption, inefficiency and wastefulness of the army appalled me. I'd been lucky to escape death or mutilation, but I'd had my brush with them and was not pleased to discover how badly it had frightened me, how fragile life is and how easily we can lose it, perhaps through nothing more than a single misstep: this was a salutary moral lesson, no doubt, but I trembled to learn it. Perhaps most shattering of all, I had lost my adolescence but found nothing to replace it. I'd become worldly but not wise: a seasoned soldier but in all other respects still an innocent boy, adroit at outwitting bureaucracy but still awkward with girls, suspicious of authority but still too inexperienced to trust my own judgment. In this I was scarcely unique, of course. This is what nations do to their young men.

The rest was routine and is quickly told. After more than thirty days at sea the *Jumper* docked at Seattle. There we went for a few days into quarters I later recognized in the background shots of the film *An Officer and a Gentleman*, and there we were sorted out by geographical regions, on the basis of which we were put on troop trains. Five days later mine pulled into the Separation Center at Fort Bragg, North Carolina, and the process of demobilization began. Though poor at waging war the army is good at moving human flesh, and the system it had devised was exact. On arrival we were told precisely when, three days later, we would be mustered out, then allowed to call our families. The procedure almost perfectly reversed the way I'd been "received" at Fort Jackson what now seemed an eternity ago; I was even "debriefed"—unlovely word—by the same sergeant, now a civilian government employee, who'd interviewed me and put me in the medics years before, though when I called his attention to the coincidence he smiled and confessed he could not remember me. We were poked and probed; we were issued new o.d. blouses and trousers and all the appropriate stripes, patches and ribbons were attached; we were paid, including accumulated back pay, and urged to join the reserves, which drew hoots but no enlistments.

Thus at last, at 9:46 on the morning of April 24, 1946—as out of the corner of my eye I saw my parents' black Buick pull up to the edge of the field and my mother hop out, no doubt to tell the army it was a minute late—I stepped up to the rostrum, saluted a bored major, got my discharge papers in return and walked down the ramp a civilian once again. My parents came forward to take me in their arms, looking grayer, careworn, greatly older, while behind them my boyhood friend Tommy snapped pictures. Then we got into the car and went home, and two weeks later, less a day, I turned twenty-one and became eligible to vote.

Composed by BookMasters, Inc.
Printed and bound by Delmar
Designed by Debra L. Hampton